LEARN TO PLAY ON
TABLA-2
(ADVANCE COURSE)

PANKAJ PUBLICATIONS

LEARN TO PLAY ON
TABLA-2
(ADVANCE COURSE)

RAM AVTAR 'VIR'
Sangeet Acharya

PANKAJ PUBLICATIONS
NEW DELHI

© PANKAJ PUBLICATION
ISBN No. : 81-87155-01-9

Tabla—II (Advance Course)

First Print 1984
Revised Edition 1998
30ᵗʰ Edition 2002

by

Pankaj Publications
M-114 Vikas Puri, New Delhi - 110018
Email : book@vsnl.com
Website : www.pankajbooks.com

Distributed in India by :
Cambridge Book Depot
3, Regal Building, Sansad Marg, New Delhi-110 001
Phone : 336 3395   Telefax : 91-11-5546260, 3348805
Email : cambridgebooks@hotmail.com

PREFACE

The Tabla instruments plays on essential role in displaying music and helps the vocalists, instrumentalists and the dancers to displays their arts in time and rhythm. Tabla is not much attractive instrument if played independently. But the tabla players please the audience with double, triple and four speeds of Thekas with Moharas Thehai, Pushkara, Rela, Lagi & Ladi Parans and Uthans etc. Playing the Tabla independently is more difficult than if it is played in the group of musicians with orchestra. The player has to make a goood practive to play the instrument independently on the stage.

We have given Thekas of Tala in different types, doubles, triples and fourths speed of various Thekas with Peshkaras, Kayadas, Parans, Lagis, Ladis and Relas in very easy and clear way. The reader can make god practive on this instgrument.

We have also given the history of Tabla with their Gharanas and their styles of playing Tabla. If the reader before practive according to this book tries to go through the first bok on Tabla, the Tabla player can get sufficient knowledge of playing Bols and Thekas and tuning the instrument.

I am confident that this book will be a great help to those who are eager to practice Tabla for Advance Course.

Ram Avtar 'Vir'
Sangeetacharya

CONTENTS

1. HISTORY OF TABLA

The percussion instruments came into practice earlier than any other musical instrument and hence this instrument remained as the basic percussion instrument. In folk songs and folk dances Dhol, Dapha and Mridang were used as the percussion instruments. With the passage of time when the classical songs became popular in Courts and Darbars, in these times too, the Mridang and Pakhawaj were played with Dhrupad and Dhamar Gayans.

In 13th Century AD, Amir Khusro, the Chief Councillor of Allauddin Khilzi invented Tabla, the new musical instrument by dividing Pakhawaj into two equal halves. This new intstrument was played by placing it in front but unfortunately it could not get any position in Royal families of those days. It limited itself upto the Kavvals, Gazal Gayaks and the dancers with them. They often performed their programmes before the soldiers etc. Tabla was the main instrument of their performances.

Now-a-days the Tabla has attained the appreciable position in standard musical societies. But in classical dances Mridang is still used.

After the invention of the Tabla instrument it was made popular by Ustad Uddar Khan. He did not produce any new bols but drew them out of the bols of Mridang according to old rules of Talas.

TEN RULES OF TALAS

The Kala, Marg, Kriya, Anga, Graha, Jati, Laya, Yati and Prastar are considered essential for the formation of Tala.

1. *Kala* : Kala is the time taken in one round of Tala divided in Matras Tali and Khali.

2. *Marg* : Type of playing Theka is called Marg.

3. *Kriya* : The practical display of Theka on Tabla of Pakhawaj is called Kriya.

4. *Ang* : The formation of Theka with their Matras and Bols is called Ang.

5. *Graha* : The starting point of a Theka is called Greh (Sam point). In olden times the Tabla player showed their capability in playing Theka and to express Sam point in different ways—Sam, Visam, Ateet and Anaghat.

Sam : In ordinary way the Tabla players show Sam point of Theka in first Matra. This way is called Sam.

Visam : The playing of Theka by keeping Sam point hidden is called Visam.

Ateet and Anaghat : When Sam point is shown before the first Matra is called the Ateet and when it is shown after the first matra it is called Anaghat.

6. In olden times 5 Jatis of Tala were popular and the matras of Thekas changed according to Jatis. Every Jati got a value of Laghu in different numbers. These were called Jatis.

7. *Kala* : The method of play an instrument is called Kala or the Art of displaying.

1

8. *Laya* : Laya is the rhythm which is used at the time of playing Theka.

9. *Yati* : The method of showing rhythm in different ways at the time of displaying Theke is called Yati.

10. *Prastar* : The expansion of Thekas with the help of Tihai, Tukada, Mohra, and Paran to make it more attractive is called Prakar.

Each of the above Tala has been expressed in 5 Jatis (categories). It means the number of Talas popular at that time consisted $7 \times 5 = 35$. The Five Jatis were as follows:-

1. Chatsar,	2. Tisar,	3. Khand,
4. Misrit,	5. Sankeerna.	

The value of matras changes with the change of matras of Laghu but Khands (bars) remain the same. The Laghu matras are as follows:-

1. Chatsar Jati	4 Matras
2. Tisar Jati	3 Matras
3. Khand Jati	5 Matras
4. Misrit Jati	7 Matras
5. Sankeern Jati	9 Matras

GHARANAS OF TABLA

In new Tala system the name of every Tala, its matras, bols, bars and the number of Tali-Khali have been fixed. They are not changed on the basis of Jatis now. Some players change the bols of Theka according to their need. But the remaining system of Theka remains the same i.e. Teen Tala of 16 matras, 4 bars, 3 numbers of Tali and 1 of Khali etc.

DIFFERENT GHARANAS OF TABLA

Delhi Gharana (Tabla) : Ustad Uddar Khan was popular musician of Delhi Darbar. hence he developed the instrument with the assistance of the Court. The style of playing and the bols which he invented are called *Delhi Baj.*

The Delhi Baj attains the prominent position in the historical evolution of Tabla. Chanti and Duggi play the essential role in playing this instrument and is mostly played with the first and second fingers of right hand. Kayadas Peshkasas, Guts and Rellas are mostly used.

Rest of the Bajs (Tabla Playing Systems) i.e. Poorva Baj, Lucknow Gharana Baj, Farukhabad Gharana Baj, Agra Gharana Baj and Punjab Gharana Baj etc. owe their origin to Delhi Baj.

Ustad Sidhar Khan was the parental source of all these Bajas.

No reliable proofs are found in the history of Tabla about the disciples of Ustad Sidhar Khan. Only three disciples named Roshan Khan, Kallo Khan and Tullan Khan and three sons named Bugara Khan, Ghasit Khan and the third unknown come in picture.

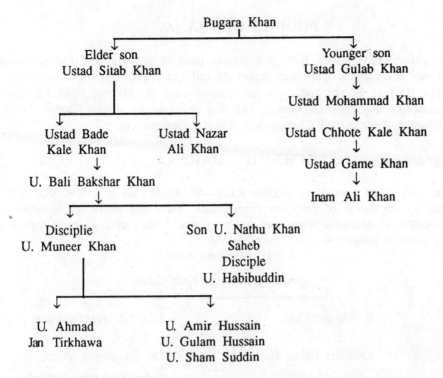

Bugara Khan

Elder son
Ustad Sitab Khan

Younger son
Ustad Gulab Khan

Ustad Mohammad Khan

Ustad Bade
Kale Khan

Ustad Nazar
Ali Khan

Ustad Chhote Kale Khan

U. Bali Bakshar Khan

Ustad Game Khan

Inam Ali Khan

Disciplie
U. Muneer Khan

Son U. Nathu Khan
Saheb
Disciple
U. Habibuddin

U. Ahmad
Jan Tirkhawa

U. Amir Hussain
U. Gulam Hussain
U. Sham Suddin

The third son of Ustad Sedhar Khan is unknown but his descendents have laid foundation of some Gharanas. He had three sons—U. Makhu Khan, U. Maudu Khan and Ustad Baksu Khan. Ustad Maudu Khan and Baksu Khan are the parental starters of Poorab Gharana.

Chand Khan was the younger brother of Ustad Sidhar Khan where descendents are represented as follows:-

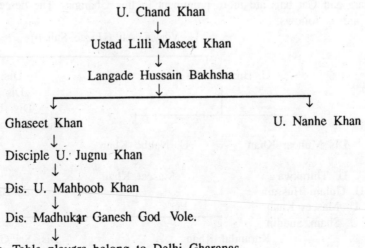

U. Chand Khan

Ustad Lilli Maseet Khan

Langade Hussain Bakhsha

Ghaseet Khan

U. Nanhe Khan

Disciple U. Jugnu Khan

Dis. U. Mahboob Khan

Dis. Madhukar Ganesh God Vole.

All the above Tabla players belong to Delhi Gharanas.

3

POORAB GHARANA

The Khule Bols (Open Bols) are mainly used in this Baj and Paran, Tukade, Nabhakkes etc. are played. This Baj is not as mild as Delhi Baj but is rather a bit forceful. The Bols of Siyahi and Palm are mainly used in this Baj. The Poorab Baj clearly expresses the Pakhawaj and dance. This Baj is played by several Gharanas such as Lucknow Gharana, Farrukhabad Gharana and Banaras Gharana etc.

LUCKNOW GHARANA

The two grand sons of U. Sodhar Khan—U. Maudu Khan and U. Baksu Khan were invited by the Navab of Lucknow from Delhi. They laid down the foundation of Lucknow Gharana. U. Mamman Khan was the prominent Tabla player of this Gharana. His descendents were as follows:—

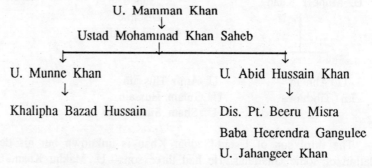

FARUKHABAD GHARANA

U. Baksu Khan got his daughter married to U. Vilayat Ali (Hazee Saheb) alongwith some knowledge of Tabla. Hence Vilayat Ali is the founder of this Gharana. Peshkara and Gat bajs are more prominent in this Gharana. The descendents of Vilayat Ali Khan are as follows:

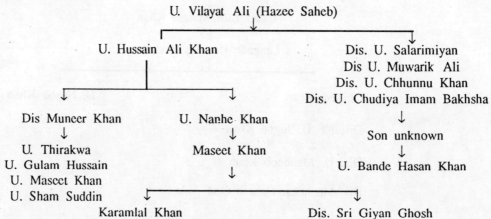

4

BANARAS GHARANA

The Banaras Gharana is also a branch of Lucknow Gharana. Pt. Ram Sahay the disciple of U. Mandu Khan has been the first musician. His descendents are as follows:—

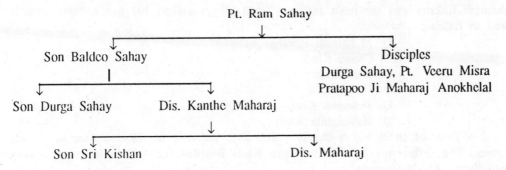

Pt. Ram Sahay

Son Baldeo Sahay

Disciples
Durga Sahay, Pt. Veeru Misra
Pratapoo Ji Maharaj Anokhelal

Son Durga Sahay   Dis. Kanthe Maharaj

Son Sri Kishan   Dis. Maharaj

Durga Sahay was though blind yet he was a famous Tabla player of Banaras Gharana. His descendents were as follows :—

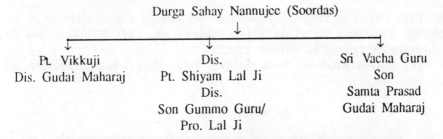

Durga Sahay Nannujee (Soordas)

Pt. Vikkuji
Dis. Gudai Maharaj

Dis.
Pt. Shiyam Lal Ji
Dis.
Son Gummo Guru/
Pro. Lal Ji

Sri Vacha Guru
Son
Samta Prasad
Gudai Maharaj

Among the Tabla players of Banaras Gharana, Pt. Pratapoo Ji Maharaj has been a prominent Tabla player. He was bestowed with the boon of Mahakali. His descendents are as follows:—

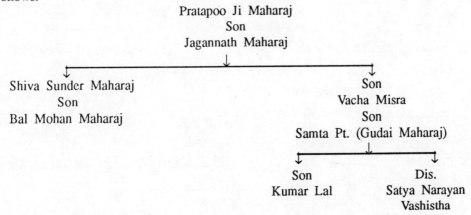

Pratapoo Ji Maharaj
Son
Jagannath Maharaj

Shiva Sunder Maharaj
Son
Bal Mohan Maharaj

Son
Vacha Misra
Son
Samta Pt. (Gudai Maharaj)

Son
Kumar Lal

Dis.
Satya Narayan
Vashistha

All the above descendents of Sri Pratapoo Ji Maharaj are the descendents of Purab Gharana.

AJRADA GHARANA

This Baj is also a branch of Delhi Gharana and has been named after a Village Ajrada in District Meerut. This Baj was started by two brothers—Kallu Khan and Meeru Khan. Both of them were the disciples of Shitab Khan, the son of U. Bugara Khan. U. Muhamadi Baksha was the most famous Tabla player among his descendents who is ranked as follows:—

U. Mohamadi Baksha
U. Chand Khan
U. Kale Khan
U. Hassu Khan
U. Shambhu Khan
U. Habibuddin Khan

A Tinge of Delhi Baj is clearly visible over the style of Tabla playing of Ajrada Gharana. The difference is only of Laya Kari. Besides the left hand is used very beautifully in Ajrada Gharana.

THE PUNJAB GHARANA

The Tabla players of Punjab Gharana have not brought any new change in system of Tabla playing. They have started the Baj of Pakhawaj on Tabla. The Guts and Parans of Punjab Gharana are famous of difficult Layakari.

U. Fakir Baksha Khan has been the first Tabla player. His descendents are as follows:-

U. Fakeer Khan
↓

Son U. Kadir Baksha Khan   Dis. U. Karam Ilahi Khan
Dis. M. Alla Rakha Saheb

2. PARTS OF TABLA

(DHAMA AND DUGGI)

Puda

Black

Kinar

Deewal

Deewal

Kumbh

Langot

Duggi   Tabla

1. *Tabla* (Right)—Kumbha (wooden drum)—It is made from a round block of sheesham wood, hollowed from inside. Its top is a small round shape and the bottom is a large round shape. Its roundness increases gradually from top to bottom.

2. *Dhama* (Left)—Kumbha (wooden drum)—It is made from the round wooden block of mango or sheesham wood, hollowed from inside. The roundness of the Dhama top and bottom is nearly the same.

3. *Duggi* (Left)—A drum made of copper or brass nickel plated from outside. The top of drum is wider than Tabla and Dhama.

4. *Pudda* (Top)—The top of Tabla, Dhama and Duggi are made of the skin of deer fastened to the leather hoops.

5. *Deewal* (Leather Brasses)—It is a long leather brasses used for the purpose of holding the top of Tabla, Dhama and Duggi over the body of the drum.

6. *Gatte* (Wooden Pegs)—'Gatte are of (7 × 3) cms. in size in a cylindrical shape. These pegs are used for tuning the Tabla. These wooden pegs are kept between the drum and the leather brasses. The total number of these pegs is eight. They are made from the sheesham or mango wood.

7. *Langot* (Leather Ring)—It is a small leather ring which is kept in the bottom of Tabla. Dhama or Duggi for holding the leather brasses joined together with the top of drum stretched with leather brasses.

3. TUNING OF TABLA

It is very essential to every Tabla player that he should be very well conversant with the exact tuning of Tabla. The untuned Tabla always confuses the mind of Tabla player and he is unable to produce harmony properly and cannot attract the audience.

THREE TYPES OF TABLA TUNING

1. The tuning of Tabla based on natural sound of drum.
2. The tuning of Tabla based on musician's basic note i.e. Shadaj (Sa).
3. Tuning of Tabla based on Madhyam (Ma) or Pancham (Pa) of musicians basic notes (Sa).
This type of tuning is called Shadaj Madhyam (Sa-Ma) and Shadaj Pancham (Sa-Pa).

The beginners of Tabla instrument should take help of harmonium for Tabla tuning. This is an easy way for them to pick up the sound of the note to tune his instrument; because the sound of Tabla should be tuned according to the sound of harmonium note.

THE TUNING OF TABLA BASED ON NATURAL SOUND OF DRUM

Every Tabla drum according to its size gives natural sound when stroken by fingers on the top (Pudda). The sound of Tabla depends upon two things:—

(a) Height of Tabla, and (b) Circumference of the top.

The Tablas having wider circumference of top and greater height produces lower pitch. On the other hand the Tablas having comparatively smaller top circumference and lesser height produced higher pitch.

THE TUNING OF TABLA BASED ON MUSICIANS BASIC NOTE i.e. SHADAJ (Sa) OR MADHYAM (Ma) OR PANCHAM (Pa)

The Tabla (right) should be tuned on the musicians fixed notes for this purpose. One can take help of Harmonium, Piano, Organ or Piano Accordian. The voice of note which is used for Tabla tuning should be kept in mind before the start of Tabla tuning, because the sound of fixed note should be produced on Tabla on every point around it equally.

Way of Tuning : For tuning a small hammer can be used. Before using the hammer, the top of Tabla should be tightened with bottom small ring by leather brasses and the pegs should be placed between drum and leather brasses. Four brasses should be kept over every peg and the total number of pegs used in Tabla is 8.

Using of Hammer : For the adjustment upto 3 notes the stroke used on pegs. When the stroke is given top to downwards, the sound should be raised and when hammer stroke is given from down to upward the sound fall down.

Tuning Points : When you want to start tuning hammer on the top, strike the Tabla top with right hand first finger and give hammer stroke with left hand and hear the sound produced. Telly it with the sound of note fixed for the tuning produced by harmonium or by any other musical instrument.

If the sound is lower than fixed note sound give the hammer stroke from upward to downward and if the sound of top is higher than tuning note sound give the hammer stroke from down to upward and check the sound by right hand first finger gradually.

Tuning of Dhama or Duggi : For tuning of Dhama only two notes should be used. The sound of notes of Tabla is the base. According to that sound the first system is Shadaj (Sa) of Mandra Saptaka of lower octave. Both the systems are used according to the choice of player and the size of duggi.

9

4. BOLS OF TABLA

The bols of Tabla have been made out from the bols of Pakhawaj and Mridang of olden times.

These bols were as follows : —

Nagan	=	III	=	KTK
Yagan	=	ISS	=	N Ta Dha
Ragan	=	SIS	=	Dha N Dha
Magan	=	SSS	=	Dha Dha Dha
Bhagan	=	SII	=	Dha K T
Tagan	=	SSI	=	Dha To N
Jagan	=	ISI	=	K Ta K
Sagan	=	IIS	=	KT Dha

OLD SYSTEM OF TALAS

All the matras of every Tala and the bars were fixed but the number of matras changed according to their Jatis. This system brought a change.

The following Seven Talas had been adopted in Indian music in olden days :—

1. Ek Tal, 2. Roopak Tal, 3. Jhap Tal, 4. Triput Tal, 5. Math Tal, 6. Dhruva Tala, 7. Ath Tala.

BOLS OF TABLA

Bols of Tabla contain 15 letters. Out of which four letters are for left hand and eleven for right.

Left hand letters :

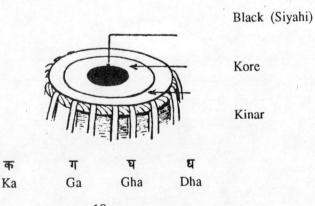

Black (Siyahi)

Kore

Kinar

क	ग	घ	ध
Ka	Ga	Gha	Dha

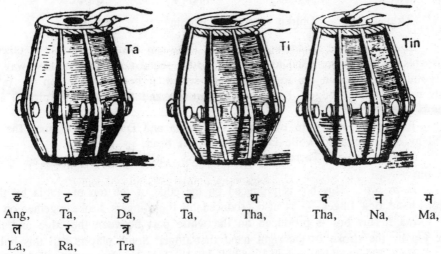

ड   ट   ड   त   थ   द   न   म
Ang,   Ta,   Da,   Ta,   Tha,   Tha,   Na,   Ma,
ल   र   त्र
La,   Ra,   Tra

Letters combined with single vowel to make words :

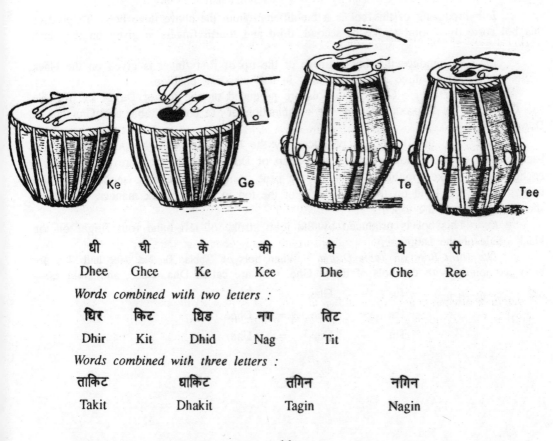

धी   ची   के   की   घे   घे   री
Dhee   Ghee   Ke   Kee   Dhe   Ghe   Ree

Words combined with two letters :

धिर   किट   धिड   नग   तिट
Dhir   Kit   Dhid   Nag   Tit

Words combined with three letters :

ताकिट   धाकिट   तगिन   नगिन
Takit   Dhakit   Tagin   Nagin

11

Words combined with four letters :

तिरकिट	धिरकिट	गिद्गिन	धुमकिट
Tirkit	Dhirkit	Gadigin	Dhumkit

How to produce sound of letters from Tabla and Dhama : Just as in other musical instruments the points are fixed to produce musical sound notes, in the same way in Tabla also points are fixed on the top to produce sound of bols. On the top of Tabla three points named Kinar (edge), Kore (white portion) and Siyahi (black circle) are to be remembered.

Tabla is divided into two parts i.e. Tabla and Duggi or Dhama. The Tabla is played by the right hand while Duggi by the left hand.

Bols on Tabla : There are seven bols on Tabla. They are produced by the right hand fingers.

Ta or Na : This bol is produced on the edge of the top of Tabla by the stroke of right hand first finger. Ta is also produced by four fingers stroke together on Tabla.

Tee : This bol is produced on the white part between the edge and the black circle top by the stroke of the right hand first finger. Some players call this bol as Ta.

Tin : This bol is produced on the black circle by the stroke of right hand first finger. It is also produced by first, second and third fingers combined strokes on Siyahi or black.

Te : Producing of this bol is a bit different from the above three bols. To produce this bol correctly a joint stroke of second, third and fourth fingers is given on the black circle.

Tay : To produce this bol a stroke of the tip of first finger is given on the black circle, the remaining three fingers are kept in half standing position.

Bols on Duggi : Only three bols are produced on the top of Duggi i.e. Ke, Ge and Ghe, Dhe bol is produced with the combination of Ta bol of Tabla and Gha bol of Duggi.

Ghe : Ge or Ghe bol is produced by the left hand with the position that the back portion of palm should rest on white part of Duggi and the pressure of arm should be light. The stroke should be given by the bent position of the first, second and third fingers of the left hand on the black circle of the top in a very quick manner. The finger should not rest on the top.

Ke : This bol is produced by the joint stroke of left hand four finger on the black circle of the Duggi.

The Joint Bols on Table Duggi : When bols of Tabla Ta, Na, Tee and Tin are produced jointly with the bols of duggi Ghe, they are called Dha, Dhee, and Dhin as:—

Ta	+	Ghe	=	Dha
Tee	+	Ghe	=	Dhee
Tin	+	Ghe	=	Dhin

5. TALA AND LAYA

(TIME AND RHYTHM)

Tala and Laya are unconscious motions of calculation which begin to stir when the impression of sounds penetrates our susceptibilities and takes a definite shape of melody and harmony form, grasping and reducing both to unifomity. This combined sense of feeling is music which rouses the organism, stimulates the currents, wakes the imaginations, links up the duration and fragments of long lost memory of space and finally acts as mediator for the harmonious combinations of manifold factors of life. Manifestly the study of Tal and Laya forces, strengthens and endures the knowledge of musical education.

Tala : In Indian music the tune element is an essential process. The regular succession of sound vibration is necessary to make sound musical. Also in vocal and instrumental music and also in dancing intervals are created to make music melodious. These intervals were created by clapping of hands and hence it is called Tala.

Pakhavaj, Mridang, Dhol, Nakkara, Duff, Khanjari and Tabla etc. are the instruments used for the purpose of Talas. Out of these musical instruments Tabla is most popular.

The late Indian musicians invented many Talas of different matras (strokes), Khands (Bars) and Bols (words) and fixed the points of 'Sam' Talis and Khalis for every Tala.

Matra (Stroke) : A matra is taken as the shortest time in which a syllable can be properly pronounced.

Bols : The sound produced by Tabla Dhama or Duggi by stroke of fingers and hand in different ways is called Bols i.e. Ta, Na, Tœ, Tin, Ke, Ge, Te, Tay, Dha, Dhe, Dhin.

Theka : The round of a Tala has fixed matras and on every matra there are fixed bols. They are called Thekas. For example Bols of Theka, Tala and Dadara (Matra 6).

Sam	×		0 Khali			
Bols	Dha	Dhin		Na	Dha	Tin	Na
							×
Matra	1	2		3	4	5	6

13

SUM, TALI AND KHALI

The system of time and rhythm of Indian music is different from that of foreign time and rhythm. In foreign music the time and rhythm of two, three or four matras are popular and they represent only the idea of stop where necessary. In the mean time the musical instruments are kept at stand still and after the stoppage-time, the orchestra starts playing.

The talas play a prominent role in the Indian folk songs and folk dances which are practiced with smaller number of matra-talas.

In the olden Indian time and rhythm only talas were practiced on bars but later on when Khayal Gayaki was introduced in music, the Khali point was included in each Tala because in Khayal Gayan the musician produces the nature of Raga by improvisation—aa—aa and further he can take help of Khali points to reach the Sum point (First stroke of Tala).

Sum—The starting point of a Tala is called Sum. Say first matra of Talas is Sum point and on every Theka it is shown by × sign.

The Sum in ordinary way means to meet or unite at a certain point. The musician and the Tabla player meet at Sum point in such a way that it produces a strange pleasure to audience and the people shout the words of pleasure—*wah—wah*—on the stroke of Sum × time. The Sum is fixed at first matra in each Tala and every Tala is started from Sum × point but there is no fixed Sam point in songs. The popular phrase or the sentence of the line of songs is repeatedly emphasised to show its prominence in the song and is linked with it afterwards.

The positon of Sam point is not definitely marked in a song on the basis of matras of Talas. It is fixed by the musician on the basis of its style and movement of words and the Tabla player starts playing Thekas from the Sam point of the musician and when the Bol of Sam of the musician and the Sam of the first Matra of the Tabla repeatedly meet together in Khayal Gayaki then it is called the Sam and strange pleasure of the union and the stroke of time and rhythm show a beautiful picture of the music.

Tali—Clapping of hands is called Tali i.e. Theka of Talas having Tali points are marked 1 2 3 4 etc.

In foreign music system the player shows the time by the movement and stroke of foot but in Indian system the Talas are no doubt counted but the movement and the stroke of foot is given on the basis of bars and not on every matra. Talis are started with Sam i.e. the clapping of hands clearly shows the bars of talas from the first matra of Tala. It gives the full idea of bars to Khayal Gayak about the Gayan (song). This knowledge of the bars helps the musician to recognise the Sam point and to join the tune or song. The Talis oin Bars play an important part in dance so evey dancer starts his dance with the help of Talis. The time bar and Talis give great pleasure of dance to the audience. In Indian music the Matras of every Tala—the position of bar, Tali and Khali are fixed and the Tabla player fixed his Tala according to the Matras of the first line of the song and starts his Tala from the Sum point. The Tala is started from the first Matra and the Sum of the musician and the same repeated Bols of musician join with Tala at Sum point and the Talis of that Sum point are given more loudly than the Talis given in ordinary way.

Khali—Khali means a gap of some matras which Bols of Theka play by right hand on Tabla only. The left (Duggi or Dhama) remains silent in Khali matras time.

Khali points help the classical musicians to understand the starting point of their Tala (Sam point) when they sing Khiyal. Khali point on Theka is shown by 0 sign.

TALA CIRCLE

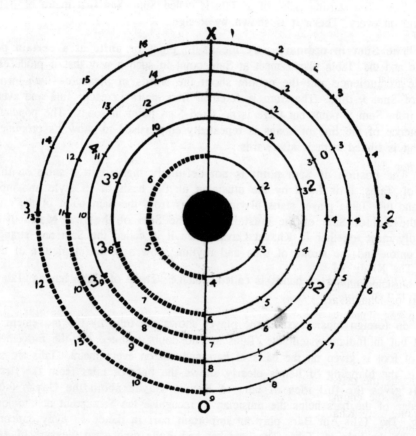

The Khali point in Northern Indian Talas is fixed after half of the total Matras in that Tala. Some Talas such as Adachautal and Sool Tala which have been formed by doing some changes in Ek Tala have difference in Khali points. The following Thekas are shown in circle Teen Tala, Talwada, Deepchandi, Chartala, Ektala, Jhap, Keharva and Dadra.

THE STATEMENT OF PREVALENT TALAS IS GIVEN BELOW :

Name of Tala	Total Matras	Half of the total Matras	No. of Matras of Khali point
Teen Tala	16	8	9
Deepchandi	14	7	8
Jhumra	14	7	8
Dhamar	14	7	8
Ek Tala	12	6	7
Char Tala	12	6	7
Jhap Tala	10	5	6
Tala Keharwa	8	4	5
Tala Dadara	6	3	4

The Khali point is very essential in Khayal Gayaki because the instrument-player and the musician recognise the Sam point of Tala, with the help of Khali point. The Bols of Duggi or Dhama are kept silent at the Khali point of Tala and the Matras of Khali point are completed by the Bols of right hand and the Bols of Duggi are stopped. The Khayal Gayak easily recognises the Khali point and after that by the help of Khali points he approaches the Sam point.

It will not be exaggerated if we suppose the Khali point as the outer railway signal just as the driver of the train gets the idea of the distance of platform and controls the speed of the engine by seeing the outer signal and reaches his destination conveniently, in the same way Khali point is few matras before Sam point. Besides there is a home signal between the platform and the outer signal which gives the exact idea of boundary of the platform. In major Talas the Khali point is far away from the Sam point and one Tali point is fixed between the Khali and Sam point to control the destination, just for example Tal Dadra. It has 6 Matras in two bars of three Matras each. Its Sam is determined on the first Matra and the Khali point is on fourth Matra. The Sam distance is of three Matras time but in big Talas just as in Teen Tala, there are 16 Matras in four bars of four Matras each. The Tali point is on first, fifth and thirteenth Matras while Khali is on the ninth. The Sam point is at the interval of 8 Matras time from Khali which is far from the Sam point. Hence one Tali point is fixed on thirteenth Matra for the convenience of musician to approach their destination (Sam point).

Tala Dadra

1	2	3	4	5	6
Dha	Dhin	Na	Dha	Tin	Na

Teen Tal

1	2	3	4	5	6	7	8	9	10	11	12	13	14	15	16
Dha	Dhin	Dhin	Dha	Dha	Dhin	Dhin	Dha	Dha	Tin	Tin	Ta	Ta	Dhin	Dhin	Dha

LAYA (Speed)

Laya (Speed)—In ordinary sense Laya means speed or any regular movement to complete a circle in a definite time. It is a natural harmonious flow of vocal and instrumental sound and also a regular succession of ascent. According to observations there are three types of speed in Indian music :

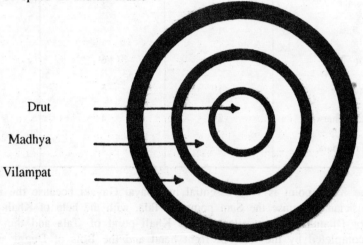

Drut

Madhya

Vilampat

     (*i*) Fast Speed (Drut Laya)
     (*ii*) Medium or Normal speed (Madhya Laya)
     (*iii*) Slow speed (Vilampat Laya)

Normal speed—Normal speed is the time required by musicians to complete a round or a circle of a part of song, tune or dance in easy way without exertion. Normal speed is the base of the remaining two speeds i.e. fast and slow speeds.

Fast speed—Fast speed means half the time or normal speed *i.e.* if a musician requires, one minute time to complete a part of songtune or dance in normal speed, he will require half of the time taken by the normal speed. In other words we can say that the musician can take two rounds of his definite part of play in time required in normal speed.

Slow speed—In slow speed a musician takes double the time to complete the round required by the normal speed. Suppose, if he completes a round of his play in one minute in normal speed, he will take two minutes to complete the same round. In medium or normal speed the time of a Matra is presumed to be one second, in fast speed half second and in slow speed—two seconds.

Types of Speed

The Tabla player uses many types of speed to bring the beauty in expression of his display according to the Indian time and rhythm. The speeds used in Indian music system are as follows :—

1. Equal speed
2. Double speed
3. Tripple speed
4. Four times speed
5. Six times speed
6. Eight times speed
7. Oblique speed
8. Kiwadi speed

1. *Equal speed :* To play every Bol of Tabla in one matra time is called the Equal speed or the speed of Dha, such as :

1	2	3	4
Dha	Dhin	Dhin	Dha

The one matra time has been supposed to be one second.

2. *Double speed :-* To play two Bols in one matra time is called the Double speed, such as:-

Dha   Dhin   Dhin   Dha

3. *Triple speed :—* To play three Bols in one matra time is called the Triple speed such as :—

Dha Dhin Dhin   Dha Dha Dhin

4. *Four times speed :—* To play four bols in one matra time is called the Four times speed such as :—

Dha Dhin Dhin Dha

5. *Six times speed :—* To play six bols in one matra time is called the Six times speed such as :—

Dha Dhin Dhin Dha Dha Dhin

6. *Eight times speed :—* To play eight bols in one matra time is called the Eight times speed as :—

Dha Dhin Dhin Dha Dha Dhin Dhin Dha

7. *Oblique speed* :— To play three bols in two matra time is called the oblique speed. In this speed the player plays his instrument in oblique way. Some players call Triple speed as an oblique speed, such as :—

Dha   Dhin   Dha
|_____|

8. *Kiwadi speed* (Double oblique speed) :— Kiwadi speed is more difficult than the oblique speed. To play 3 bols in two matra time or 5 bols in 3 matra time is called the Kiwadi speed.

6. HOW TO PRACTISE

The practice of Tabla is not much interesting. Some times it makes one monotonous and un-interesting but this instrument is the soul of music because music cannot be given perfection without time and rhythm. Hence the Tabla player should make a regular practice of about two hours daily. Rhythm is the base of time, hence, one should take a great care of the movement of hand and fingers whether they are rhythmical or not. The practice should be done in following manner :—

1. The number of bols to be produced on Tabla and Duggi alongwith the movement of fingers on them.
2. To assemble the bols i.e. to play two bols, three bols and four bols together.
3. The practice of the Theka of Tabla alongwith its Duggan, Tiggan and Chaugan etc.
4. The practice of playing Mohra, Mukhada types of Gats, Paran and Rela etc.

The details of bols of Tabla and Duggi along with movements of hand and fingers is illustrated for guidance.

21

7. DEFINITION OF WORDS USED IN TABLA PLAYING

Prakar	— To play on Theka in different styles.
Peshkar	— To display various styles of bols of Theka in different rhythms. It shows the bols of Theka in single, double, triple and quadruple rhythms.
Kayada	— The group of bols of Tabla played in different styles with various combinations.
Rela	— To play bols of Tabla in different styles in fast speed i.e. Quadruple and Double Quadruple speed.
Raw	— Raw is also a kind of Rela with the difference that Raw is played in small parts of Theka i.e. in two, three or four matras.
Palla	— To play bols of Rela and Kayada combined and separate in different styles to produce new variety.
Gat	— Gat is the combination of bols played in different rhythmic styles and shows clearly both Khali and Tali points. This style is popular in Banaras, Poorab and Punjab Bajs.
Kayada Gat	— To play Gat on Kayada style is called Kayada Gat and is popular in Delhi Baj.
Chakardar Gat	— The bols of Theka or Gat played in Triple speed starting from Sam and taking three rounds and meet at Sam point again are called Chakardar Gat.
Tripalli Gat *(Triple Gat)*	— The Gat in which the bols of single, double and triple rhythms are played combined is called the triple gat.
Chaupali Gat	— The bols Theka of Teen Tala having 16 matras if divided in four parts having 4 matras each to play each part separately in different style and rhythm, it is called the Chaupali Gat.
Mukhada	— The opening bols of Tabla to pick point of Sam for starting Theka is called Mukhada.
Mohra	— The starting bols of Tabla to follow tune displayed by the dancer, singer and the instrument player to pick Sam point for starting Theka.

styles of the bols in different rhythms like a Paran before starting the Theka is called **Uthan**.

Paran	— Paran is the chief method of playing Pakhawaj by taking four or five rounds of Theka and coming back to the Sam point along with Tiya.

The bols of Theka after being played three times to complete the circle, meet at Sam point again are called Tiya or Tihai.

Gharana	— The system of learning Tabla by any Guru or teacher is called Gharana or Baj i.e. as Delhi, Agra, Lucknow Gharanas etc.
Bant	— There are two opinions regarding Bant (i) To play the bols of Theka in different types (ii) Bols of Theka played in different rhythms.
Laggi	— The bols of Keharwa, Dadra, Pasto and Roopak Talas played in different styles are called Laggi.
Ladi	— Ladi is the method of playing Tabla by linking the bols together side by side. It is also called Ladaut.
Sangat	— Sangat is the method of playing Tabla adjusting the dancer, singer and instrument player to have a beautiful display of their programme.
Thah (Dugan)	— The slow speed is called Thah or Vilampat Laya and playing of Tabla in Double speed from Thah laya is called Dugan.
Tigun and Chaugan	— The uniform speed played in Triple and Quadruple speeds are called Tiguns and Chaugans.
Aad and Kwad	— The uniform speed if played in one and a half the speed is called Aad and if again doubled it is called Kwad.

On the basis of Matras Tihai is of three types :

(i) Four Matra's Tihai

(ii) Eight Matra's Tihai

(iii) Sixteen Matra's Tihai

Parans are also of many types :—

(i) *Kamal Paran* — The Parans which are played on Banaras Gharana in Poorab Baj are called Kamal Parans.

(ii) *Chakardar Parans* — The piece of a Gat after being played four or five rounds of the Theka and meets at Sam point is called Chakardar Paran.

(iii) *Farmaishi Paran* — The Paran which are played on the demand of the audience are called Farmaishi Parans.

Lalkila Parans	— The Parans which are played on the style of Nakkaras and Shahnais played in Mughal period are called Lalkila Parans.

Lalkila Parans	— The Parans which are played on the style of Nakkaras and Shahnais played in Mughal period are called Lalkila Parans.
Char Bagh	— Relas and Parans when played on the basis of one special Bol to display clear picture in every round are called Char Bagh.
Chalan	— Chalan means a particular system of starting Tabla in different States and Gharanas.
Biad and Pauri Layas	— The uniform speed of playing Tabla is played 1/4 times is called Biad i.e. normal speed + 3/4 of it adding together are called Biad.

8. THEKAS OF TABLA

The Pakhawaj and Mridang were the popular musical instrument in olden days. Their bols were played on different styles of dance. The same bols continued to be used in Tabla when it came into practice but as the time passed they were modified little by little. In Muslim period the Tala was divided into two system Northern system and the Southern system.

In Sourthern system the movement of Talas remains uniform with a change of number of Matras in bars. These Talas are of five categories. The number of Matras in Guru remains fluctuating.

In the Talas of Northern system were fixed the Matras, Bars, points of Tali and Khali along with Bols. Some musicians made changes in Bols of Thekas but did not make any change in Matras, Bars and points of Tali and Khali.

On the basis of Bols of Thekas the Northern system differs from Southern system not only in number of Matras but also in the type of playing Thekas.

The Thekas of Northern system were formed in Muslim period and the Bols of Thekas were fixed according to the manner of movement of birds and animals. If we play the Bols of Thekas according the manner of movement, every Theka shows its own type of rhythm.

The movements of horse, donkey, elephant, deer and camel among the animals and peacock and dove in birds, resemble more with Talas. In Muslim rule some Talas were formed on the basis of the movement of these birds and animals. The movement of some Talas is given as follows:

Teen Tal : It contains 16 Matras in four Bars of four Matras each. One Khali and three Tali points are given. Bols are as follows:

THEKA TAL TEEN

+				2				0				3			
1	2	3	4	5	6	7	8	9	10	11	12	13	14	15	16
Na	Dhee	Dhee	Na	Na	Dhee	Dhee	Na	Na	Tee	Tee	Na	Na	Dhee	Dhee	Na

The movement of this Theka follows the movement of horse. The horse walks with regular time in every step. In race too, the time of steps remains regular and uniform.

The Teen Tala also resembles with the movement of horse. This Theka is considered as the best one because of the use of four Matras in each bar.

Some musicians compare Teen Tal with the movement of railway train. The railway track contains joints. When

the train passes over the track, the joints produce a Tik, Tik sound. As the joints are found in the lines at alternative intervals, so when the wheels of the train move over these joints they produce a regular sound. Besides when the train starts from the station passing over various crossings to reach the main line it appears as if some Table player might be playing Mohra and Mukhada before reaching the Sam point.

When the train reaches the platform through home signal, the Parans and Relas of Teen Tala are felt at the time when the train is between the home signal and the platform because of the fast speed.

Hence the comparison of Teen Tala with that of railway train is not unsuitable.

TALAS OF 14 MATRAS

The popular movements of this category are Deepchandi, Jhumra, Dhamar and Adachautal, out of which the first three are related with Hori which is a special festival celebrated all over India. This is also called a seasonal festival. It occurs at the end of winter season. According to the Indian system of seasons it actually falls in autumn which is a season of mild days. Hence people celebrate it with great activity, enthusiasm, singing, dancing and throwing coloured water upon one another in groups in lanes and streets of villages, towns and cities.

Deepchandi and Jhumra are the rural Talas. The folk songs are generally sung in these Talas. Tala Dhamar is used in songs of royal families and is more concerned with Hori songs of higher category. The emperors, queens, princes and the maid servants generally celebrate Hori on this Tala.

THEKA TAL DEEPCHANDI

x			2				0			3			
1	2	3	4	5	6	7	8	9	10	11	12	13	14
Dha	Dhin	—	Dha	Ge	Tin	—	Ta	Tin	—	Dha	Ge	Tin	—

THEKA TAL JHUMRA

x			2				0			3			
1	2	3	4	5	6	7	8	9	10	11	12	13	14
Dhin	Dhin	Nak	Dhin	Dhin	Dhage	Tirkit	Tin	Tin	Nak	Dhin	Dhin	Dhage	Tirkit

THEKA TAL DHAMAR

x					2		0			3			
1	2	3	4	5	6	7	8	9	10	11	12	13	14
Ka	Dhee	Ta	Dhee	Ta	Dha	—	Ge	Ti	Ta	Ti	Ta	Ta	—

THEKA TAL ADA CHAUTAL

×		2		0		3		0		4		5	
1	2	3	4	5	6	7	8	9	10	11	12	13	14
Dhin	Trik	Dhin	Na	Too	Na	Kat	Ta	Trik	Dhin	Na	Dhin	Dhin	Na

Ada Chautal — Ada Chautal contains 14 matras but differs from Deepchandi, Jhumra and Dhamar in manner of movements. This Tala of 14 matras resembles with that Chartal of 12 matras. The Ada Chautal was formed by the Dhrupad Musicians by adding two matras in Chartal. The Ada Chautal so formed started to take the place of Dhamar Horis of royal families.

TALAS OF 12 MATRAS

The popular Talas of 12 matras are:—
(a) Ektala   (b) Chartala.

Ektala is generally used in Khayal Gayan. The Bada Khayals are specially sung on this Tala. The movement of this Tala is deep and in slow rhythm and is mainly sung in Vilambit laya. The movement of this Tala resembles with the walk of elephant. Every Bol is clearly depicted by the slow and steady movement of the musician. The slow movement of the Tala is responsible for the clear understanding of the art of music in Khayal Gayan to understand the Sam point.

THEKA TAL EK TALA

×		0		2		0		3		4	
1	2	3	4	5	6	7	8	9	10	11	12
Dhin	Dhin	Dhage	Tirkit	Too	Na	Kat	Ta	Dhage	Tirkit	Dhin	Na

Char Tala—This is played more with Dhrupad Gayan. The movement of this Tala in Dhrupad Gayan resembles with the walk of elephant, but when dhrupad gayan is sung in double, triple, fours and eights the Tabla player starts to play in Allied Bols (Sath Ke Bols) and on account of fast speed the Allied Bols loosing the nature of movement of elephant, resemble more with the race of deer whereas the musician sings his songs leaping from one note to another.

27

THEKA TAL CHAR

×		0		2		0		3		4	
1	2	3	4	5	6	7	8	9	10	11	12
Dha	Dha	Din	Ta	Kit	Dha	Din	Ta	Tit	Kat	Gadi	Gina

TALAS OF 10 MATRAS

Two popular Talas of Ten Matras are : (a) Jhap Tala, (b) Sool Tala.

Jhap Tala resembles with that of a camel and the musician moves up and down like a man riding on a camel. The manner of sitting on a camel indicates the Matras of this Tala. The keeping of knees on ground by bending the forelegs, should be considered as the first Matra. The putting on the behind right leg forward should be taken as the second Matra. The movement of left leg is the third Matra. Sitting on ground by the behind legs is the fourth Matra. He takes the complete sitting with the help of fifth foot. The fifth foot is the additional one and remains attached with the breast. In standing too he takes help from it. Hence the style of sitting and standing both represent manner of Jhap Tala. The Jhap Tala contains the ten Matras having two bars of two Matras each and two bars of three Matras each as follows :

THEKA TAL JHAP

×		2			0		3		
1	2	3	4	5	6	7	8	9	10
Dhin	Na	Dhin	Dhin	Na	Tin	Na	Dhin	Dhin	Na
Dhee	Na	Dhee	Dhee	Na	Tee	Na	Dhee	Dhee	Na

When Dhee and Na are played on the Tabla it appears as some man is walking swinging his body forward and backward. This is the style of man riding on a camel.

Sool Tala is formed by cutting two Matras from Char Tala and contains ten Matras in 5 bars of two Matras each. The movement of this Tala resembles with that of Dove hence some musicians call Sool Tala as Dove or Sool Fakhta.

THEKA TAL SOOL

×		0		2		3		0	
1	2	3	4	5	6	7	8	9	10
Dha	Dha	Din	Ta	Kit	Dha	Tit	Kat	Gadi	Gina

28

TALAS OF 8 MATRAS

The Talas of Eight Matras are played in light and folk songs. This Tala resembles more with the walk of donkey who is a poor and simple animal. Before learning horse riding, children start riding from donkey. The donkey can very easily go through hill and plain, straight and narrow curved paths. Tala Keharwa like the walk of donkey is played in every type of song having different number of Matras—two, four or eight.

The other style of this Tala which is more easier in dancing of four matras. The peacock when dances gayfully, he takes four steps rightwards and turns back to the starting point and again taking four steps leftward and again comes on its original place. Tala Keharwa suits every type of dance and song, folk or light.

THEKA TAL KEHARWA (8 Matras)

×				0			
1	2	3	4	5	6	7	8
Dha	Ge	Na	Tee	Ta	Ke	Dhin	Na

THEKA TAL KEHARWA (4 Matras)

1	2	3	4
Dhin	Dha	Tin	Na
Dhage	Nake	Take	Dhina

THEKA TAL KEHARWA (2 Matras)

×	
1	2
Dhage	Nak

29

TALA OF 6 MATRAS

This type of Tala is the Tal Dadra which is represented by a pigeon picking up the food grains. When the pigeon picks up one grain he looks sidewards and moves one or two paces forward and repeats the same thing again. In this way the picking up of grains, looking sidewards and steping forward etc. complete the three matras. Both the parts of three matras of Tala dadra move in the same manner. It makes the song beautiful and attractive.

THEKA TAL DADRA

×			0		
1	2	3	4	5	6
Dha	Dhin	Na	Dha	Tin	Na

IInd Type

Dha	Dhin	Dha	Dha	Tin	Ta

9. THEKAS OF TALAS

(THEKA TAL DADRA 6 MATRAS)

This Theka is used in Gazals, Bhajans, Geets, Thumaree and Dadra etc. The movement of this tala is like that of a jumping bird.

It contains 6 matras in two bars of three matras each having Tali and Sam on first matra and Khali on fourth.

×			0		
1	2	3	4	5	6
Dha	Dhin	Dha	Dha	Tin	Ta

IInd Type

Dha	Dhin	Na	Dha	Tin	Na

Duggan Tal Dadra

×			0		
1	2	3	4	5	6
Dha Dhin	Dha Dha	Tin Ta	Dha Dhin	Dha Dha	Tin Ta

Tiggan Tal Dadra

×			0		
1	2	3	4	5	6
Dha	Dhin Dha	Dha Tin Ta	Dha Dhin Dha	Dha Tin Ta	Dha Dhin

Chauggan Tal Dadra

1	2	3
Dha Dhin Dha Dha	Tin Ta Dha Dhin	Dha Dha Tin Ta
4	5	6
Dha Dhin Dha Dha	Tin Ta Dha Dhin	Dha Dha Tin Ta

31

Uthan

×			0		
1	2	3	4	5	6
Dhage	Tina	Kidang	Tirkit	Takta	Kittak
Dhage	Tina	Kidang	Tirkit	Takta	Kittak

Tihai Tal Dadra

×			0		
1	2	3	4	5	6
Tit	Kat	Dha	Aa	Dha	Tit
Kat	Dha	Aa	Aa	Kit	Kat Dha

IInd Type

Tirkat	Kidang	Dha	Aa	Tirkat	Tirkat
Kidang	Dha	Aa	Aa	Tirkit	Kidang Dha

1.	Dhatrak	Dha Dha	Dhinna	Tatrak	Dha Dha	Dhinna
2.	Dhagenadha	Dhinna Ginna	Trak Dhinna	Takenata	Tinnakinna	Traktinna
3.	Dhak Dhin	Nak Dhin	Dhin Dhin	Nagtrak	Teenkat	Dhingin
	Taktin	Naktin	Teen Teen	Naktrak	Teenakit	Tin Kin
4.	Dhage	Teena	Taktatirkit	Taketeena	Kidangtirkit	Taktatirkit
		Kidangtirkit				
5.	Dhagin-nadhee	Adhingindha	Dhinna Tirkit	Takinnatin	Tinkin-Ta	Tinnatirkit

Peshkara (Tala Dadra)

1.	Dhatee	Dha Dha	Dhinna	Tatee	Dha Dha	Dhinna
2.	Dhatee	Dha Dha	Dhina	Dhati	Dha Dha	Dhinna
	Tatee	Tata	Tinna	Dhatee	Dha Dha	Dhinna
3.	Dhati	Dha Dha	Tirkit	Dhati	Dha Dha	Dhinna
	Tatee	Tata	Tirkit	Dhati	Dha	Dhinna
4.	Dhati	Dha Dha	Tirkit	Dhinna	Ginna	Tirkit
	Tatee	Tata	Tirkit	Tinna	Ginna	Tirkit
5.	Dhatee	Dha Dha	Tirkit	Tatee	Tata	Tirkit
6.	Dhatee	Dhage	Dhinna	Ginna	Tirkit	Dhatee
	Tatee	Take	Tinna	Ginna	Tirkit	Dhatee
7.	Dhatee	Dhinna	Tirkit	Dhati	Dhinna	Tirkit
	Tatee	Tinna	Tirkit	Dhatee	Tinna	Tirkit
8.	Tirkit	Dhatee	Dha Dha	Tirkit	Dha Dha	Dhinna
	Tirkit	Tatee	Tata	Tirkit	Dha Dha	Dhinna

32

9.	Tirkit	Dhatee	Dhatee	Ginna	Tirkit	Dhatee
	Tirkit	Tatee	Tatee	Ginna	Tirkit	Dhatee
10.	Dha Dha	Adha	Tirkit	Dhin	Dhatee	Gin
	Tata	Sta	Tirkit	Dhin	Dhatee	Gin

Laggi and Ladi Tala Dadra

1.	Dhage	Dheena	Gin	Tage	Teena	Kin
2.	Dhage	Dheena	Gin	Dhage	Dheena	Gin
	Take	Teena	Kin	Dhage	Dheena	Gin
3.	Dhage	Dhinna	Ginna	Tage	Dhinna	Ginna
4.	Dhinna	s Dha	Tirkit	Tinna	s Dha	Tirkit
5.	Dhage	Dhinna	Tirkit	Tage	Dhina	Tirkit
6.	Dhak	Dhinna	Tirkit	Take	Tinna	Tirkit
7.	Dhinna	s Dha	Tirkit	Dhage	Na Dha	Ginna
	Tinna	s Ta	Tirkit	Dhage	Na Dha	Ginna
8.	Dhinna	s Dha	Ginna	Tinna	s Ta	Tirkit
9.	Dhakit	Takta	Kittak	Takit	Takta	Kittak
10.	Dhakit	Takta	Kittak	Dhage	Dheena	Gin
	Takit	Takta	Kittak	Dhage	Dheena	Gin

THEKA TALA ROOPAK 7 MATRAS

This Theka being of Seven Matras is called half of Deepchandi but it differs in movement. This type of Thekas are played generally in Bhajans and Geets etc. It contains seven matras of Tala, 3 bars of Tala (one, three and two matra), 3 Talees (on 1, 4 and 6), —as Khalees of Talee and the same on first matra. There is another theka of same matras called Teevra.

Bols of Theka—Tala Roopak

0			2		3	
1	2	3	4	5	6	7
Te	Te	Na	Dhe	Na	Dhe	Na

Bols of Theka—Tala Tivra

Dha	Dhin	Ta	Tit	Kat	Gadi	Ginna
×			2		3	

Duggan Tala Roopak

Dhin Dha	Trik Dhin	Dhin Dha	Trik Dhin	Dhatrik	Dhin Dhin	Dhatrik

Tiggan Tala Roopak

Te Te	Na Dhe	Na Dhe	Na Te	Te Na	Dhe Na	Dhe Na
Te	Te	Na	Dhe	Na	Dhe	Na

Chaugan Tala Roopak

I	II	III	IV	V
Dhin	Dhin	Dhin	Dha	Dha
	VI	VI		
	Trik	Trik		

Chaugan Tala Roopak

x	2	3	x
Dhin Dhin Kit Tak Dha Aa	Dhin Dhin Kit Tak Dha	Aa Dhin Dhin Kit Tak	Te

Prakar Tala Roopak

1. Teekra	Teetee	Natrak	Dhee	Nana	Dhee Dhe	Na
2. Tœ Tee	Natrak	Tinna	Dhe Dhe	Natrak	Dhee Dhee	Na Na
3. Dheen	Kridheen Dhee	Tirkit	Dha	Krinatin	Dha Dha	Teena
4. Tœ Tin	Kinta	Tinta	Dhin Dha	Tit Dhin	Dha Dha	Dhin Na
5. Teen	Kirnatin	Tirakit	Taa	Kirnattin	Dha Dha	Teena

Peshkara Tala Roopak

0				1		
1. Tage Nate	Tittin	Tatatin	Dhati ta Dha	Dhin Dha Dha	Dhita Dhin	Dha Dha
2. Tittage	Natatirkit	Tirkittak	Ghidan	Dha Dha Dha	Titghe Ghe	Nak Dhin
3. Tagente	Tirkitin	Tatakin	Dhitdhage	Nadha Tirkit	Ghaghetirkit	Tirakittak
4. Tittata	Tirkittin	Tirkitta	Dhina s Dha	Tirkit Dhin	Dhadhatirkit	Taktatirkit
5. Tatakin	Tikkin	Tirkit ta	Ghighinak	Dhadha s Dha	Dhagendha	Tirkitdhin
6. Dhinna	Kridhan	Dhinna	Kridhan	Dhagan-dha	Kittakdhin	Gintak
Tinne	Kritan	Tinna	Kritan	Dhagen-dha	Kit tak dhin	Gintak
7. Dhagtrak Skra	Dhigagin Dhindha	Dheekra Tirkit	Dhindha Dhingin	Tirkit Skra	Dhagtrik Dhindha	Dhingin Tirkit
8. Dhinna Tinna	Dhee Dhee teenteen	Natrak Natrak	Dhagtikik Dhagtirkit	Dhinagina Dhinagina	Dheen Dheen	Dheen Dheen

34

9.	Dhadheena	Kitdhag	Trakteena	Kittak	Teenakit	Dhagtrak	Teenakit
	Tateena	Kittak	Trakteena	Kittak	Teenakit	Dhagtrak	Teenakit
10.	Dhee	Dheena	Kata	Dhudhe	Nadhee	Dheena	Tirkit
	Tee	Teena	Kata	Teetee	Nadhee	Dheena	Tirkit

TALA KEHARWA MATRAS 8

Like Tala Keharwa two other thekas of same matras i.e. Dhumali and Kavvali are more popular in Indian music. They are played with Geets, Bhajans, light songs and dances.

They contain 8 matras, two bars of 4 matras each, one tali and one khali. Sam is on first matra.

Tala Keharwa is played in 8 matras, 4 matras and 2 matras.

THEKA TALA KEHARWA MATRA 8

×				0			
1	2	3	4	5	6	7	8
Dha	Ge	Na	Tee	Na	Ke	Dhin	Na

THEKA TALA KEHARWA MATRAS 4

	×			
1.	Dha	Dha	Dhag	Nak
2.	Dha	Ge	Na	Ke

THEKA TALA KEHARWA MATRAS 2

×	
Dhag	Nak

Duggan of Tala Keharwa

	×				0			
1.	Dhage	Natee	Take	Dhinna	Dhage	Natee	Take	Dhinna

THEKA TALA DHUMALI MATRAS 8

×							
Dha	Dhin	Nat	Tin	Tirak	Dhin	Dhage	Tirak

Duggan of Theka Tala Dhumali

×						0			
Dhadhin	Natin	Trik	Dhin	Dhage	Trik	Dhadhin	Natin	Trikdhin	Dhagetrik

35

THEKA TALA KAVVALI MATRAS 8

×				0			
Dha	Dhin	Dha	Dha	Tin	Tin	Dha	Dha

Duggan of Theka Tala Kavvali

×				0					
Dhadhin	Dhadha	Tin Tin	Dha Dha	Dha Dhin	Dha Dha	Tin Tin	Dha Dha

THEKA TALA JHAP MATRAS 10

This theka is played with chhota Khayal, Geet and Bhajans etc. Its movement resembles with that of camel. It contains four bars of two matras each and two of three matras each and possesses three Tali point and one Khali point. Sam is on first matra.

Bols of Theka Tala Jhap
(1)

×		2			0		3		
1	2	3	4	5	6	7	8	9	10
Dhee	Na	Dhee	Dhee	Na	Tee	Na	Dhee	Dhee	Na

(2)

×		2			0		3		
Dhee	Dhee	Trak	Dhee	Na	Tee	Tee	Trak	Dhee	Na

(3)

Dheen	Tirakit	Dhee	Na	Dheen	Tirakit	Teen	Tirakit	Dhee	Na

Dhuggan of Theka Tala Jhap

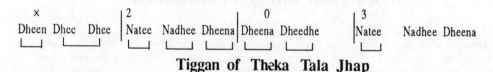

×			2			0		3		
Dheen	Dhee	Dhee	Natee	Nadhee	Dheena	Dheena	Dheedhe	Natee	Nadhee	Dheena

Tiggan of Theka Tala Jhap

×		0			
1	2	3		4	5
Dheena Dhee	Dheenaten	Nadhindhin		Nadheena	Dheedheena
Teenadhee	Dheenadhee	Nadheedhee		Nateena	Dheedheena

36

Chaugan of Theka Tala Jhap

Dheenadheedhee	Nateenadhe	Dheena Dheena	Dhadheenatee	Dadheedheena
Dheena dhee dhee	Nateenadhe	Dheena Dheena	Dhe Dheenatee	Nadhee Dheena

Tukade Tala Jhap

	0		3		
1.	Dhagentir	Kitdhage	Tirkit	Dhadha	Tirkit
			2		
2.	Nagteena	Kidnagtatir	Kittaktirkit	Taktatirkit	Dhatirkittak

Mukhade Tala Jhap

× 2 0

1. Dheen Deen Titakit Gheghere tit Gheghedun Dheenkra Dhan Dhan Ghakra Dhan Dhan
   Dhakra   Dhan Dhan
2. Dhetta   Dhit tit Kradhe Aatdha Ginakidnag   Tirakittakdhir Kittakdhati
   Dha Aadhir Kittakdhatee Dha Aadhir Kittakdhati

Tihai Tala Jhap

	×		2			0		3		
1.	Dhagtir	Kit-tak	Dha	Aa	Dhagtir	Kit-tak	Dha	Aa	Dhagtir	Kit-tak
2.	Dhadha	Tirkit	Dha	Aa	Dhadha	Tirkit	Dha	Aa	Dhadha	Tirkit
3.	Tirkit	Kdan	Dha	Aa	Tirkit	Kdan	Dha	Aa	Tirkit	Kdan

Prakar Tala Jhap

	×		2			0				
	1	2	3	4	5	6	7	8	9	10
1.	Dheen Nana		Dheekra	Dheedhee	Nana	Teen	Nana	Dheekra	Dheedhee	Nana
2.	Dhee Nana		Dheekra	Dheedha	Nana	Teetee	Nana	Dheekra	Dheendheen	Nana
3.	Dhee	Dheedhee	Nana	Dheedhee	Nana	Teen	Teen teen		Nana	Dheedhe Nana
4.	Dhee	Tirakit	Dhee	Dheena	Tirkit	Teeka	Teenteen	Dhadha	Dheekra	Dhindhin
5.	Dheen	Tirkit	Dhee	Na	Dhee	Teen	Teentage	Natatirkit	Dhee	Na

Preshkara Tala Jhap

×
1. Dhadha Dhinna Dhatee Dhadha Dhindha Dhadha Dhindha Dhatee
   Dhadha   Dhindha
   Tata Tinta Tatee Tata Tinta Dhadha Dhindha Dhatee Dhadha Dhindha
2. Tikitak Ginta Aa Aa Dhatee Aadha Teedha Tinta Tateen Tata Tinta
3. Dhatrak Dhadhatrak Dhinnaadha Tirakitdhadha Dhinnatit Trak tinna

Dhindha Dhatrak Tintit Trakdhin
Tatrak Tatatrak Tinna Aadha Titadhadha Dhinnatit Tintrak Teenagin
Dhagendha Gegegege Trakdhindha

4. Dheekdhindha Dhagendheedheenak Aadhadindha Dhikitatgen Dhateedhatee Kittakteen
Titatinteenagin Titaghidnag Dhatitdhage Dhadhadhindha

5. Tirakit Dhadha Dindha Tirakit Dhadha Dhindha Dheeka Dhindha
Aadha Dhindha

Titatita Tinta Trakteen Teentrak Dhindha Dheekra Dhindha Aadha
Dhindha Dhadha

Kayada Tala Jhap
(1)

1. Dhintrak Dhingin Dhageteena Trak Dheena Gintrak Dhindhage Dhagendha Aadhagen
Trakdhin Teenagin

2. Dhingin Trakdhin Gintrak Dhagtrak Dhingin Dhgendha Gindhage
Trikdhage Dhingin Dhagetrak
Tinkin Traktin Kintrak Tagtrak Dhingin Dhagendha Gindhage
Trakdhage Dhingin Dhagetrak

3. Dhidnag Tirktit Takdha Teedha Gin Dhage Dhinna
Trak Dhinna Gin
Dhatee Dhage Nadha Teedha Gin Dhage Tit Kridha Tit Ghidan
Kidnag Tirakit Takta Teeta Kin Tage Tinna Trak Dhinna Gin
Dhatee Dhage Nahda Teedha Gin Dhage Tit Kridha Tit Ghidan

4. Trakdhinna Ginnatrak Dhagetit Trakdhin Gindhage Nadha Aadha Trakdhinna
Dhagetit Dhagedhinna Ginnatrak Traktinna Ginnatrak Tagetit Traktin
Kintrak Nadha Aadha Trakdhinna Dhagdit Dhagidhinna Dhinnatrak

5. Tirakitdhati Dhagendha Teedhagin Dhateegin Teedhagin Tirkittati Takentra
Teeitakin Dhateegin Teedhagin

(2)

1.	Dhatir	Kittak	Dhatir	Kittak	Dhinna	Ginna	Dhatir	Kittak
	Tatir	Kittak	Tatir	Kittak	Tatir	Kittak	Dhinna	Ginna
	Dhatir	Kittak	Tatir	Kittak				
2.	Dhatir	Ghirnag	Taktit	Ghirnag	Taktit	Ghirnag	Dhatir	
	Ghirnag	Tinna	Gina	Tatir	Kirnag	Taktir	Kidang	
	Taktir	Kidnag	Dhatir	Ghirnag	Tina	Ginna		
3.	Kidnag	Tirkit	Tagtir	Kittak	Dhatit	Ghidnag		
	Dhatir	Ghidnag	Tinna	Kidnag	Kidnag	Tirkit		
	Taktir	Kittak	Dhatit	Ghidnag	Dhatir	Ghidnag	Tina Kidnag	
4.	Dhadha	Tirkit	Tirkit	Taktir	Kittak	Tirkit	Dhatir	
	Kittak	Dhatir	Kittak	Taktir	Kittak	Taktir	Kittak	
	Dhatir	Kitdha	Tirkit	Tak	Dhatir	Tirakit	Tata	
	Tirkit	Tirkit	Tirkit	Kittak	Tirakit	dhatir		
	Kittak	Dhatir	Tirkit					

38

THEKA EK TALA MATRAS 12

This tala is played with Bada Khayal Gayakis. The other form of 12 matras theka is named Chartal which is played with Dhrupad Gayan.

It contains 12 matras divided in 6 bars of two matras each. It has four Tali and two Khali Points. Its Sam is on first matra.

×		0		2		0		3		4	
1	2	3	4	5	6	7	8	9	10	11	12
Dhin	Dhin	Dhage	Tirkat	Too	Na	Kat	Ta	Dhage	Tirkat	Dhin	Na

Duggan Theka Tala Ek

Dhin Dhin Dhage Tirkit Toona Katta Dhage Tirkat-Dhinna Dhindhin Dhage Trakat Toona Katta Dhage Tirkit Dhinna

Tiggan of Theka Tala Ek

×			0			2		
1	2	3	4	5	6			
Dhin	Dhin Dhage	Tirkit Toona	Katta Dhage	Tirkit Dhinna	Dhin Dhin Dhage	Tirkit Toona		

		3		4		
7	8	9	10	11	12	
Katta Dhage	Tirkit Dhinna	Dhindhin Dhage	Tirkit Toona	Katta Dhage	Tirkit Dhinna	

Chaugan of Theka Ek Tala

Dhin Dhin Dhage Tirkit Toona Katta Dhage Tirkat Dhinna Dhin Dhin Dhage Tirkit Toona Katta Dhage Tirkit Dhinna
Dhin Dhin Dhage Tirkit Toona Katta Dhage Tirkit Dhinna Dhin Dhin Dhage Tirkit Toona Katta Dhage Tirkit Dhinna

THEKA CHAR TALA MATRAS 12

×		0		2		0		3		4	
Dha	Dha	Dhin	Ta	Kit	Dha	Dhin	Ta	Kit	Tak	Gidi	Ginna

Duggan Theka Char Tala

Dhadha Dinta Kitdha Dinta Gidgina Dhadha Dinta Kitdha Dinta Kittak Gidgina

Tiggan Theka Char Tala

Dhadhadhin	Takit Dha	Dintakit	Nakgidi Ginna	Dhadhadhin	Takitdha
Dintakit	Nakgidgina	Dhadadhin	Takitdha	Dintakit	Nakgidgina

39

Chaugan Theka Chartal

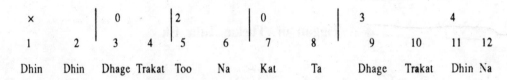

×		0			2	
1	2	3	4		5	6
Dhadhadinta	Kitdhadinta	Kittakgidgina	Dhadhadinta		Kit dha dinta	Kit tak gid gina

		3		4	
7	8	9	10	11	12
Dhadhadinta,	Kitdhadinta	Kittakgidgina	Dhadhadinta	Kitdhadinta	Kittakgidgina

Theka Ek Tala

×		0		2		0		3		4	
1	2	3	4	5	6	7	8	9	10	11	12
Dhin	Dhin	Dhage	Trakat	Too	Na	Kat	Ta	Dhage	Trakat	Dhin	Na

Tihai Theka Ek Tala

1. Dhagtit Dhagtit Dha Da Da Dhagtit   Dhagtit   Dha Aa Aa Dhagtit   Dhagtit
2. Dhatirkit Tatirkit Dha Aa Aa Dhatirkit   Tatirkit Tak Dha Aa Aa Dhatirkit   Tatirkit

Peshkar Theka Ek Tala

×	0	2	3	3	4

1. Dhit, Dhagadha, Dhindha, Dhati, Dhadha, Dhindha, Tinna, Takala, Tinta, Dhati, Dhadha, Dhindha.
2. Dhit, Dhagadha, Dhindha, Dhit, Dhagadha, Dhindha, Tit, Takata, Tinta, Dhit, Dhagadha, Dhindha.
3. Dhit, Dhagadha, Dhit, Dhagadha, Tirakit, Dhindha, Tita, Takata, Tit, Dhagadha, Tirakit, Dhindha.
4. Dhit, Dhagadha, Dhindha, Dhati, Dhadha, Dhin, Dha, Dhit, Dhagadha, Dhindha, Dhati, Dhadha, Dhindha.
   Tit, Takata, Tinta, Tati, Tata, Tinta, Dhit, Dhagadha, Dhindha, Dhati, Dha, Dha, Dhindha.
5. Tirakit, Dhit, Dhagadha, Tirakit, Dhit, Dhagadha, Tirakit, Tit, Takata, Tirakit, Dhit, Dhagadha.

Kayada Theka Ek Tala

1. Dhag, Tit, Dhag, Nag, Tina, Katta, Tag, Tit, Dhag, Nag, Tina, Kata.
2. Dhagtit, Dhagtit, Dhagnaga, Teena Katta, Dhagnag, Teena Katta, Nagtit, Tagnag,
   Dhagnag, Teenakatta, Dhagnag, Teenakatta.

40

3. Dhagtit, Dhagnag, Teena Kaita, Dhagnag, Teena Katta, Dhagtit
   Nagtit, Tagnag, Teena Katta, Dhagnag, Teenakatta, Dhagtit.

4. Dhagtit, Dhagnag, Teena Katta, Dhagtit, Dhagnag, Teena Katta, Tagtit, Tagnag, Teena
   Katta, Dhagtit, Dhagnag, Teena Katta.

5. Dhagnag, Teena Katta Dhagtit, Dhagnag, Teena Katta, Dhagtit, Tagnag, Teenakatta,
   Tagtit, Dhagnag, Teenakatta, Dhagtit.

Paran Theka Ek Tala

1. Tirakit, Takta, Kittak, Taktir, Kittak, Tirkit, Takta Kittak, Tirakit, Takta, Kittak, Tirakit

2. Kittak, Tirakit, Takta, Tirakit, Takta, Kittak, Tagtir, Kittak, Tirkit, Takta, Tirkit

3. Kdan, Tirakit, Takta, Tittak, Dha, Tirakit, Takta, Titatak, Dha, Tirakit, Takta, Kittak.

TALA DHAMAR MATRAS 14

Dhamar, Deepchandi, Jhumara, and Adachautal contain 14 matras each but there is a difference in their bars and the positions of Tali and Khali and that difference is indicated by the signs of Tali and Khali on every Theka of Tala. Sam of every Tala is on first matra. The thekas of Dhamar, Deepchandi and Jhumara are used in Hori Gayan while Aada Chautal in Hori Dhrupad.

THEKA TALA DHAMAR MATRAS 14

×			2		0			3			
1	2	3	4	5	6	7	8	9	10	11	12	13	14
Ka	Dhi	Ta	Dhi	Ta	Dha	Aa	Ga	Ti	Ta	Ti	Ta	Ta	Aa

Duggan of Theka Tala Dhamar

×					2		0						
Kadhi,	Tadhi,	Tadha,	Aaga,	Tita	Tita	Tada	Kadhi	Tadhir	Tadha	Aaga	Tita	Tita	Ta Aa

Tiggan of Theka Tala Dhamar

×						2	
1	2	3	4	5	6	7
Kadhita	Dhatidha	Aagati	Tatita	Ta Aaka	Titadhi	Tadha Da
0			3			
8	9	10	11	12	13	14
Gatita	Titata	Dagati	Tadhita	Dha Daga	Titati	Tata Aa

41

Theka Tala Deepchandi

×			2				0			2			
1	2	3	4	5	6	7	8	9	10	11	12	13	14
Dha	Dhin	Aa	Dha	Ge	Tin	Aa	Ta	Ta	Aa	Dha	Ge	Tin	Aa

Duggan of Theka Tala Deepchandi

×			3			
1	2	3	4	5	6	7
Dhadhin	Aadha	Getin	Asta	Tin Aa	Dhage	Dhin Aa
0			3			
8	9	10	11	12	13	14
Dhadhin	Aadha	Getin	Aata	Tin Aa	Dhage	Dhin Aa

Tiggan of Theka Tala Deepchandi

×			2			
1	2	3	4	5	6	7
Dhadhin Aa	Dhagetin	Aatatin	Aadhage Dhin Aa	Dha Dhin Aa		Dhagetin Aa
0			3			
8	9	10	11	12	13	14
Tatin Aa	Dhagedhin	Aadhadhin	Aadhage Tin Aata		Tin Adha	Gedhin Aa

THEKA TALA JHUMARA MATRAS 14

×			2				0			2			
1	2	3	4	5	6	7	8	9	10	11	12	13	14
Dhin	Dhin	Nak	Dhin	Dhin	Dhage	Trikat	Tin	Tin	Nak	Dhin	Dhin	Dhage	Trikat

Duggan of Tala Jhumara

×			2				
1	2	3	4	5	6	7	
Dhindhin	Akdhin	Dhindhage	Trikat Tin	Tin Nak		Dhin Dhin	Dhage Trikat
0			3				
8	9	10	11	12	13	14	
Dhindhin	Nakdhin	Dhindhage	Trikadatin	Tirnak		Dhindhin	Dhage Trikat

THEKA TALA AADA CHAUTALA MATRAS 14

+		2		0		3		0		4		0	
1	2	3	4	5	6	7	8	9	10	11	12	13	14
Dhin	Trik	Dhin	Na	— Too	Na	Ka	Te	Trik	Dhin	Na	Dhin	Dhin	Na

42

Duggan of Theka Aada Chautta

x		2		0		3
1	2	3	4	5	6	7
Dhintrik	Dhinna	Toona	Katta	Trikdhin	Nadhin	Dhinna
	0		4		0	
8	9	10	11	12	13	14
Dhintrik	Dhinna	Toona	Katta	Trikdhin	Nadhin	Dhinna

Tihai Aada Chautal

1. Tita, Kittak, Ta, Kittak, Dha, Tita, Kit Tak, Ta, Kit-tak, Dha, Tita, Kit-tak, Ta, Kit-tak.

2. Titkat, Gadgin, Dhatit, Dhatit, Dha, Titkat, Gadgin, Dhatit, Dhatit, Dha, Titkat, Gadgin, Dhatit, Dhatit

3. Dhadhadha, Tirakitta, Dhadhinakat, Dhadhinarol, Dha Aa, Dhadhadha, Tirakitta, Dhadhinakat Dhadhirakat, Dha Aa, Dhadhadha, Tirakitta, Dhadhinakat, Dhateerakat.

4. Kittak, Tirakit, Nagatak, Tirakit, Dha, Kit Tak, Tirakit, Nagnag, Tirakit, Dha, Kittak, Tirakit, Nagtak, Tirakit.

5. Tikdan, Dhatit, Dhatirkit, Dhatit, Dhadhadha, Tikdan, Dhatit, Dhaorkit, Dhatit, Dhadhadha, Tikdar Dhatit, Dhatirkit, Dhatit.

Tookade Aada Chautal

1. Dha, Dhadha, Dheen, Dheendheen, Tirakit, Nagnag, Tirakitta.

2. Nagnag, Tirakit, Takta, Tirakit, Kittak, Gidan, Teena.

3. Gidan, Tirakit, Nagtak, Tirakit, Tata Dhidan, Dhati.

4. Dhagige, Dhagetit, Kridhe Aa, Dhatit, Dhatuna, Dhintadan, Nagdhetta.

5. Ghidnag, Dhadha Kridha, Titatita, Dhirdhirkit tak, Tatirkit tak, Dhadhadhadha, Nag nag nag nag.

Peshkar Aada Chautal

1. Dhati, Dhadha, Dhindha, Dhati, Dhati, Dhadha, Dhindha
   Tali Tate Tinta Dhali Dhati Dhadha Dhinda

2. Dhag, Dhatia, Dhindha, Dhati, Dhati, Dhindha,
   Tak, Tati, Tinta, Dhati, Dhati, Dhadha, Dhindha.

43

3. Dhagena, Dha, Dhagena, Dhadha, Dhindha, Dhati, Dhadha, Dhati, Dhadha, Aadha, Tita, Dhagena, Dhadha, Dhin dha, Takena, Ta, Takena, Tata, Tinta, Tati, Tata, Dhati, Dhadha, Aadha, Tita, Dhagna, Dhagna, Dhadha, Dhindha.

4. Dhadha, Dhindha, Dhati, Dhadha, Dhindha, Dhati, Dhati, Dhadha, Aadha, Dhindha, Dhag, Dhati, Dhadha, Dhindha, Tata, Tinta, Tati, Tata, Dhadha, Aadha, Dhindha, Dhag, Dhati, Dhadha, Dhindha.

5. Dhati, Dhadha, Dhindha, Aagheghe, Nakdin, Dhadha, Dhindha, Tati, Tata, Tinta, Aagheghe, Nakdhin, Dhadha Dhindha.

Kayada Aada Chautal

1. Takdhin, Dhagendha, Dhagitirkit, Teenagin Trakatak, Teenagin, Takdhin, Dhagendha, Dhagitinkat Teenakin, Dhirkitdha, Dheenagin Dhagetrak, Dheenagin.

Takteen, Takenta, Taketrakit, Teenakin, Traktak, Teenakin, Tak Dhen, Dhagendha, Dhagetrakit, Teenakin, Dhirakitdha, Dheenagin, Dhagetrak, Dheenagin.

2. Katakadhi, Nagtak, Dhatrakiddhee, Naktak, Dhatrakdhit, Dhitdhirkittak, Dhitdhirkittak, Katakatin, Naktak, Dhatir Kitdhani, Naktak, Dhatrakdhit, Dhitdhirkittak, Dhit Dhir Kittak.

3. Dhagtit, Dhintin, Dhatidhage, Nadhalit, Dhinteena, Dhatidhage, Nadhatit, Nagtit, Teenakin Tatitage, Nadhatit, Dhinteena, Dhatidhage, Nadhatit.

4. Dhatrak, Nakdhi, Katakadho, Naktak, Dhivdhivkittak, Tatirkittak, Katakadhi, Naktak, Dhatrakadhi, Naktak, Dhagheghe, Nakdhin, Dhirdhirkit tak, Tatir kit tak, Tatrakali, Naktin, Katakati, Naktaka, Tirtirkit tak, Tatir kit, Katakati, Nuk tak, Dhatrakadhi, Nakataki, Dhagheghe, Nakdhin, Dhir dhir kit tak, Tatir kit tak.

5. Dhin gin, Dhagtrak, Dhindhag, Dhindhag, Titdhag, Trakdhin, Dhagatit, Ghingin, Tirgin, Takrak, Tintag, Titdhag, Trakdhin, Dhagtit, Dhingin.

Rela Aada Chautal

1. Dhatit, Kintadha, Tirakit, Dhidnag, Tirakit, Ghidnag, Tatit, Kitdha, Tirakit, Dhatit, Dhidnag, Tirakit, Dhidnag.

2. Dhatit, Ghidnag, Teena Kidnag, Dhatit, Ghidnag, Tirakit, Tati, Kidnag, Teena, Kidnag, Dhatit, Dhidnag, Tirakit.

3. Dhatit, Dhidnag, Teena, Kidnag, Dhatit, Ghidnag, Dhatit, Ghidnag, Teena Kidnag, Dhatit Dhidnag, Teena, Kidnag, Tatit, Kidnag, Teena, Kidnag, Tatit, Kidnag, Tatit, Ghidnag, Teena, Kidnag, Dhatit, Ghidnag, Teena, Kidnag.

4. Dhatit, Ghidnag, Aatit, Ghidnag, Aatit, Ghidnag, Titaghid, Nagtit, Ghidnag, Teena, Dhatit, Ghidnag, Teena, Kidnag, Tatit, Ghidnag, Aatit, Kidnag, Aatit, Kidnag, Titaghid Nagtit, Ghidnag, Teena, Dhatit, Ghidnag, Teena, Kidnag.

5. Dhadha, Ghidnag, Tak, Ghidnag, Takghid, Nagtak, Ghidnag, Tirakit, Dhatit, Ghidnag, Takghid, Nagtak, Teena Kidnag, Ta Aa, Kidnag, Tak, Kidnag, Takkid, Naktak Kidnag, Tirakit, Dhatit, Ghidnag, Takghid, Nagtak, Teena, Kidnag.

TAL TEEN MATRAS 16

Theka Teen Tal contains 16 Matras having 4 bars of 4 matras each with 3 Talis and 1 Khali point, Sam being on first Matra. On account of regular movement of Matras and Rhythm this Theka is more popular. The movement of this Theka is more popular and is compared with that of horse. This Theka is played with Chhote Khayals and Bhajans.

The two more popular Thekas of 16 Matras are Talwara and Punjabi and are played with Bada Khayal.

THEKA TAL TEEN MATRAS 16

×				2				0				3			
1	2	3	4	5	6	7	8	9	10	11	12	13	14	15	16
Dha	Dhin	Dhin	Dha	Dha	Dhin	Dhin	Dha	Dha	Tin	Tin	Ta	Ta	Dhin	Dhin	Dha

Duggan of Tal Teen

×							
1	2	3	4	5	6	7	8
Dhadhin	Dhindha	Dhadhin	Dhindha	Dhatin	Tinta	Tadhin	Dhindha
9	10	11	12	13	14	15	16
Dhadhin	Dhindha	Dhadhin	Dhindha	Dhatin	Tinta	Tadhin	Dhindha

Tiggan of Tal Teen

1	2	3	4	5	6
Dhadhindhin	Dha Dhadhin	Dhindhadha	Tintinta	Tadhindhindha	Dhadhadhin
7	8	9	10	11	12
Dhindhadha	Dhindhindha	Dhatintin	Tatadhin	Dhindhadha	Dhindhindha
13	14	15	16		
Dhadhindhin	Dhadhatin	Tintata	Dhindhindha		

45

Chaugan of Tal Teen

1	2	3	4	5
Dhadhindhindha	Dhadhindhindha	Dhatintinta	Tadhindhindha	Dhadhindhindha
6	**7**	**8**	**9**	**10**
Dhadhindhindha	Dhatintinta	Tadhindhindha	Dhadhindhindha	Dhadhindhindha
11	**12**	**13**	**14**	**15**
Dhatintinta	Tadhindhindha	Dhadhindhindha	Dhadhindhindha	Dhatintinta
16				
Tadhindhindha				

MUKHRA TAL TEEN MATRAS 4

	1	2	3	4
1.	Dhadha	Titkit	Dhadha	Titkit
2.	Tikad	Tinna	Tikad	Tinna
3.	Dhadha	Teena	Dhadham	Dhadham
4.	Dhatit	Dhatit	Dhadha	Titkit
5.	Dhindhin	Ta Aa	Titkit	Gidighina

MUKHRA TAL TEEN MATRAS 8

	1	2	3	4	5	6	7	8
1.	Dhage	Tinna	Kidnak	Tatir	Kittak	Tirkit	Takta	Kittak
2.	Tirkit	Nagtar	Kidnag	Tigtar	Kidnag	Tirkit	Taktar	Kidtak
3.	Tirkit	Takta	Kittak	Nagtar	Kittak	Tirkit	Dhindam	Dhadha
4.	Kittit	Dhadhin	Tana	Kidnak	Tirkit	Nagtag	Tirkit	Dhadha
5.	Ta	Tinna	Kidnak	Tinna	Trikdhi	Natrik	Dhina	Tirkit

TEHAI TAL TEEN MATRAS 8

	1	2	3	4	5	6	7	8	9
1.	Gadi	Ghina	Dha	Gadi	Ghina	Dha	Gadi	Ghina	Dha
2.	Dha	Tirkit	Dha	Dha	Titkit	Dha	Dha	Tirkit	Dha
3.	Dhadha	Tirkit	Dha	Dhadha	Tirkit	Dha	Dhindha	Tirkit	Dha
4.	Ta	Tirkid	Dhadha	Ta	Tirkad	Dhadha	Ta	Tirkad	Dha
5.	Dhin	Dhin	Ta	Dhin	Dhin	Ta	Dhin	Dhin	Dha

TEHAI TAL TEEN MATRAS 16

	1	2	3	4	5	6	7	8	9	10	11	12	13	14	15	16
1.	Tit	kat	gade	gina	Dha	S	Tit	Kat	Gadi	gina	Dha	S	Tit	kat	gadi	gina Dha

2. Dha Tir Kit Tak Dha S Dha Tirkat Tak Dha S Dha Tirkit Tak Dha Dha

3. Kat Tirkit Kat Dha S Kat Tirkit Kat Dha S Kat Tirkit Kat Dha S Dha

4. Kat Tirkit Kat Dha S Kat Tirkit Kat Dha S Kat Tir Kit Kat

5. Dhedhe Ta S Dhedhe Tirkat Dha S Dhedha Ta S Dhedha Tirkit Dha S
   Dhedhu Ta S Dhedhe Tirkit Dha.

1	2	3	4	5	6	7	8	9
6. Dhit	Dhit	Dhitdhit	Kadan	Dha	S	Dhet	Dhet	Dhetdhit
10	**11**	**12**	**13**	**14**	**15**	**16**		
Kadam	Dha	S	Dhat	Dhet	Dhitdhit	Kadam		

1	2	3	4	5	6	7	8	9
7. Kidnag	Tirkit	Nagtag	Tirkit	Dha·	S	Kidnag	Tirkit	Nagtag
10	**11**	**12**	**13**	**14**	**15**	**16**		
Tirkit	Dha	S	Kidnag	Tirkit	Nagtak	Dha		

1	2	3	4	5	6	7	8	9
8. Tirkit	Takta	Kittak	Tirkit	Dha	S	Tirkit	Takta	Kittak
11	**12**	**13**	**14**	**15**	**16**	**17**	**18**	
Tirkit	Dha	S	Tirkit	Takta	Kittak	Tirkit	Dha	

9. Titkat Gadigina Dhati Dha S Tirkit Gadigina Dhati Dathi Dha S Titkat Gadigina
   Dhati Dhati Dha

10. Dhinkdhi Nakdhidhi Nakdhin Dhati Dha S Dhinakdhi Nakdhadha Nakdhin Dhati
    Dha S Dhinakdhi Nakdhindhi Nakdhin Dhati Dha S

PARKAR TAL TEEN

	1	2	3	4	5	6	7	8
1.	Dha	Dhin	Dhindhi	Dha	Dhadha	Dhin	Dhindhin	Dha
	Dha	Tin	Tintin	Ta	Tata	Dhin	Dhindhin	Dha
2.	Dha	Dhin	Dhindhin	Dha	Dhindhin	Dha	Dhindhin	Dha
	Dha	Tin	Tintin	Ta	Tintin	Ta	Dhindhin	Dha
3.	Dha	Dhinkad	Dhindhin	Dhadha	Dhikad	Dhindhin	Dhadha	Dhin
	Dhor	Tirkad	Tintin	Tata	Tirkad	Dhindhin	Dhadha	Dhin
4.	Dha	Dhadha	Dhindha	Dhindha	Dha	Kridhin	Dha	Dha
	Tata	Tin	Ta	Tintin	Ta	Kridhin	Dha	
5.	Dha	Dhin	Dhagindha	Tirkitdhin	Dhadha	Dhindhin	S Dha	Dhindha
	Dhatin	Tignat	Tirkititin	Tala	Dhindhin	Dhintrkad	S Dha	Dhindha

6. Tirkit Dhin Dha Trik, Tak Dhin Dhin Tirkit Tin Trik Teena Tirkit Dhin Trik
   Dhin Dha

7. Dhadha   Dhagindha Trikitdhin Dhindha S Dha Tirkitdhin Dhagindha
Tirkittin Tata, Tagenati, Taktrik Tintin Dhadhinak, Dhudhinak Dhadha Dhurdha

8.	Dhatit	Dhatit	Dhadhin	Dha	S Dha	Dhadhin	Dha	Dhindha
	Tatit	Tatit	Tatin Ta	S Dha	Dhadhin	Dha	Dhindha	
9.	Dhadha	Dhin	Dha	Dhin	Dha	Dhadha	Dhindha	
	Ta	Tintin	Tatatin	Dha	Dhindhin	Dhadha	Dhin	
10.	Dha	Tirkit	Dhin	Tirkit	Dhindhin	Dhadha	Dha	Dhin
	Dha	Tirkit	Tin	Tarkat	Tintin	Dhadha	Dha	Dhin

Peshkara Tal Teen

1.	Dhage	Dhatin	Dhadha	Dhundhin	Dhadha	Dhati	Dhadha	Dhundhi
	Turkit	Girnag	Tata	Tinta	Dhadha	Dhati	Dhadha	Dhindha
2.	Dhage	Dhati	Dhadha	Dhindha	Dhadha	Tirkat	Dhindha	Dhate
	Take	Tirkit	Tata	Tinta	Dhadha	Tirkat	Dhindhi	Dhate
3.	Dhindha	Dhati	Dhadha	Dhindha	Dhate	Dhate	Dhadha	Dhindha
	Tinta	Tati	Tati	Tinta	Dhati	Dhati	Dhadha	Dhinta
4.	Dhakad	Dhindha	Dhadha	Dhindha	Dhadha	Dhukad	Dhadha	Dhinta
	Dhadha	Tirkad	Tata	Tinta	Tirkad	Dhadha	Dhakad	Dhuta
5.	Dhadhin	Dhadha	Dhir	Nakdhin	Dhadha	Nakdhin	Dhadha	Dhin
	Tata	Tirkad	Takdhin	Tata	Nakdhin	Dhadhin	Dhadha	Dhin

Kayada Tal Teen

1.	Dhage	Tirkit	Dhage	Tirkit	Dhage	Tirkat	Tinna	Gin
	Tagi	Tirkit	Tagi	Tirkit	Dhage	Tirkit	Dhina	gina
2.	Dhin	Dhage	Nadha	Tirkit	Dhage	Tirkit	Tinna	gin
	Tin	Tage	Nata	Tirkit	Dhage	Tirkit	Dhin	gin
3.	Dhin	Dhin	Dhage	Nadha	Tirkit	Dhin	Dhin	Dhage
	Tin	Kin	Tage	Nata	Tirkit	Dhin	Dhin	Dhage
4.	Dhage	Nadha	Tirkit	Dhage	Dhin	Dhage	Nadha	Tirkit
	Tage	Nata	Tirkit	Tage	Dhin	Dhage	Nadha	Tirkit

5.	Dhagendha	Tirkitdhage	Dhagenadhi	Nagdhin
	Takdhin	Gintirkit	Dhinadhidhi	Nagdhin
	Tagenat	Tirkitgeta	Taginati	Naktin
	Takdhin	Gintirkit	Dhindhindhi	Nakdhin

THEKA TALA TALWADA MATRAS 16

1	2	3	4	5	6	7	8	9	10	11	12	13	14	15	16
Dha	Tirkit	Dhindhin	Dha	Dha	Dha	Tin	Tin	Ta	Tirkit	Dhin	Dhin	Dha	Dha	Dhin	Dhin

DUGGAN TALA TALWADA MATRA 16

1	2	3	4	5	6	7	8
Dhatirkit	Dhindhin	Dhadha	Tintin	Tatirkit	Dhindhin	Dhadha	Dhandhin
9	10	11	12	13	14	15	16
Dhatirkat	Dhindhin	Dhadha	Tintin	Tatirkit	Dhindhin	Dhadha	Dhadhin

CHAUGAN TALA TALWADA MATRA 16

1	2	3	4
Dhatirkitdhin	Dhindhadha	Tintinta	Trikatadhindhin
5	6	7	8
Dhadhadhin	Dhindhatirkit	Dhindhindha	Dhatintin
9	10	11	12
Tatirkatdhin	Dhindhadha	Dhindhindha	Tirkitdhindhin
13	14	15	16
Dhadhatin	Tintatirket	Dhindhindha	Dhadhindhin
1	2	3	4
Dhatirkitdhindhin	Dhadhatintin	Tatirkitdhindha	Dhadhadhindhin
5	6	7	8
Dhatirkitdhindhin	Dhadhatintin	Tatirkitdhindhin	Dhadhadhindhin
9	10	11	12
Dhatirkitdhindhin	Dhadhatintin	Tatirkitdhindhin	Dhadhadhindhin
13	14	15	16
Dhatinkardhindhin	Dhadhatintin	Tatirkitdhindhin	Dhadhadhindhin

BOLS OF 27 THEKAS
(Popular and Unpopular Talas)
Theka Tal Keharwa

		×		2			
Matra 2 =		Dhag		Nag			
		× 1	2	3	4		
Matra 4 =	1.	Dha	Gi	Na	Ke		
	2.	Dhagin	Tinakdhin	Tagin	Tinakdhin		
	3.	Dhage	Nake	Take	Dhina		
		×1	2	3	4	5	6	7	8
Matra 8 =		Dha	Ge	Na	tee	Ta	Ke	Dhin	Na

49

THEKA TAL DO MATRAS 5

×				
Dhin	Dhinnak	Tak	Dhin	Na
1	2	3	4	5

THEKA TAL DADRA MATRAS 6

×		0			
1	2	3	4	5	6
1. Dha	Dhin	Na	Dha	Tin	Na
2. Dha	Dhin	Dha	Dha	Tin	Na

THEKA TAL ROOPAK MATRAS 7

×			2		3	
1	2	3	4	5	6	7
1. Dhin	Dha	Trik	Dhin	Dhin	Dha	Trik
2. Tee	Tee	Na	Dhi	Na	Dhi	Na
3. Ta	Thum	Na	Dham	Kit	Gidi	Gin

THEKA TAL TEEN MATRAS 7

×			0			
1	2	3	4	5	6	7
Dha	Dhin	To	Tit	Kat	Gadi	Gina

THEKA TAL PASHTO MATRAS 7

×			0			
1	2	3	4	5	6	7
Ta	Ke	Dhin	Dha	Dha	Dha	Dhin

THEKA TAL MOL MATRAS 8

1	2	3	4	5	6	7	8
Kit	Tat	Tit	Ta	Aa	Dhit	Dhit	Dha

THEKA TAL NUSRAK MATRAS 9

1	2	3	4	5	6	7	8	9
Dhin	Na	Dhage	Tirkit	Dhin	Gin	Tin	Tin	Ta

50

THEKA TAL JHAP MATRAS 10

	1	2	3	4	5	6	7	8	9	10
1.	Dhi	Na	Dhi	Dhi	Na	Ti	Na	Dhi	Dhi	Na
2.	Dhi	Dhi	Trik	Dhi	Na	Ti	Ti	Trik	Dhi	Na

THEKA TAL SULFAKHTA MATRAS 10

	1	2	3	4	5	6	7	8	9	10
1.	Dha	Dha	Dhin	Ta	Kit	Dha	Tit	Kit	Gadi	Gina
2.	Dhin	Dhin	Dha	Tirkit	Dhin	Dhin	Dha	Tirkit	Tin	Na

THEKA TAL KUMBHA MATRAS 11

1	2	3	4	5	6	7	8	9	10	11
Dha	Dhid	Tik	Tat	Dha	Dhid	Nak	Tat	Kat	Gad	Gin

THEKA TAL EK MATRAS 12

1	2	3	4	5	6	7	8	9	10	11	12
Dhin	Dhin	Dhin	Tirkit	To	Na	Ka	Ta	Dhage	Tirkit	Dhin	Na

THEKA TAL CHAR MATRAS 12

Dhan	Dha	Dhin	Ta	Kit	Dha	Dhin	Ta	Kit	Tak	Gadi	Gina

THEKA TAL KHEMTA MATRAS 12

1	2	3	4	5	6	7	8	9	10	11	12
Dha	Te	Dhe	Na	Te	Ne	Ta	Te	Dhe	Na	Te	Ne

THEKA TAL FARDOST MATRAS 13

1	2	3	4	5	6	7	8	9	10	11	12	13
Dhagi	Tirkit	Nagi	Tirkit	Titta	Tirkit	Dhin	Dha	Dhindhin	Dha	Ge	Nag	Ghin

THEKA TAL ADA CHAUTAL MATRAS 14

1	2	3	4	5	6	7	8	9	10	11	12	13	14
Dhin	Tick	Dhin	Na	Tu	Na	Ka	Ta	Trik	Dhin	Na	Dhin	Dhin	Na

THEKA TAL DHAMAR MATRAS 14

1	2	3	4	5	6	7	8	9	10	11	12	13	14
Ka	Dhi	Ta	Dhi	Ta	Dha	Aa	Ga	Ti	Ta	Ti	Ta	Ta	Aa

THEKA TAL DEEPCHANDI MATRAS 14

1	2	3	4-5	6	7	8	9	10	11-12	13	14
Dha	Dhin	Aa	Dhage	Tin	Aa	Ta	Tin	Aa	Dhage	Tin	Aa

THEKA TAL JHUMRA MATRAS 14

1	2	3	4	5	6	7	8	9	10	11	12	13	14
Dhin	Dhin	Nak	Dhin	Dhin	Dhage	Thid	Tin	Tin	Nek	Dhin	Dhin	Dhage	Tirkit

THEKA TAL CHANCHAL MATRAS 14

1	2	3	4-5	6	7	8	9	10	11-12	13	14
Dhin	Dhin	In	Dhage	Tin	In	Na	Tin	In	Dha Ge	Dhin	In

THEKA TAL TEEN MATRAS 16

	1	2	3	4	5	6	7	8	9	10	11	12	13	14	15	16
1.	Dha	Dhin	Dhin	Dha	Dha	Dhin	Dhin	Dha	Dha	Tin	Tin	Ta	Ta	Dhin	Dhin	Dha
2.	Na	Dhi	Dhi	Na	Na	Dhi	Dhi	Na	Na	Ti	Tina	Na	Na	Dhi	Dhi	Na
3.	Dha	Takit	Dhin	Dhin	Dha	Dhin	Dhin	Dha	Dha	Tirkit	Tin	Ta	Ta	Dhin	Dhi	Dha
4.	Dha	Dhin	Tirkit	Dha	Dha	Dha	Dhin	Tirkit	Dha	Tin	Tirkit	Ta	Tirkit	Dhin	Dhin	Dha

THEKA TAL TALWADA MATRAS 16

1	2	3	4	5	6	7	8	9	10	11	12	13	14	15	16
Dha	Takit	Dhin	Dhin	Dha	Dha	Tin	Tin	Ta	Tirkit	Dhin	Dhin	Dha	Dha	Dhin	Dhin

THEKA TAL PUNJABI MATRAS 16

1	2	3	4	5	6	7	8	9	10	11	12	13	14	15	16
Dha	Aa	Dhinag	Dha	Dha	Aa	Dhinag	Dha	Dha	Aa	Tinak	Dha	Dha	Aa	Dhinag	Dha

THEKA TAL RUDRA MATRAS 17

1	2	3	4	5	6	7	8	9	10	11	12	13	14	15	16	17
Dha	Dhid	Na	Dhid	Nak	Dham	Kit	Dhid	Nak	Nak	Dhum	Kat	Tak	Dhum	Kit	Gad	Gin

THEKA TAL ASHT MANGAL MATRAS 22

1	2	3	4	5	6	7	8	9	10	11
Dha	Aa	Dhe	Na	Ke	Ta	Ta	Ta	Dhin	Na	Ke

12	13	14	15	16	17	18	19	20	21	22
Ta	Dhin	Na	Ti	Ta	Ka	Ta	Ge	Dha	Ga	Na

THEKA TAL POORAN MATRAS 23

1	2	3	4	5	6	7	8	9	10	11	12
Dha	Aa	Dha	Ke	Ta	Ke	Ta	Dhe	Na	Ta	Dhi	E
13	14	15	16	17	18	19	20	21	22	23	
Dhi	E	Ta	Aa	Ta	Ke	Ta	Ke	Tee	Ta	Aa	

THEKA TAL NAKSHATER MATRAS 27

1	2	3	4	5	6	7	8	9	10	11	12	13	14
Dha	Dhin	Nak	Tak	Dhin	Nak	Dha	Kit	Tak	Dhum	Kit	Tak	Tig	Dhin
15	16	17	18	19	20	21	22	23	24	25	26	27	
Nag	Tag	Dhin	Na	Nirdham	Tag	Nag	Take	Tidha	Kit	Shran	Dhram	Dha	

THEKA TAL ASAVARI MATRAS 30

1	2	3	4	5	6	7	8	9	10	11	12	13	14	15
Dhi	Ta	Ke	Dhi	Ta	Ke	Dhi	Dhi	Na	Ke	Dhi	Dhi	Ta	Ka	Ti
16	17	18	19	20	21	22	23	24	25	26	27	28	29	30
Na	Ti	Na	Nir	Kit	Dha	Na	Dhi	Dhi	Na	Dhi	Dhi	Na	Dhi	Na

THEKA TAL SAVARI MATRAS 32

1	2	3	4	5	6	7	8	9	10	11	12	13	14	15	16
Dhi	E	Na	Aa	Dhi	E	Dhi	E	Na	Aa	Dhi	Dhi	Na	Dhi	Dhi	Na
17	18	19	20	21	22	23	24	25	26	27	28	29	30	31	32
Tin	Tirkit	Tin	Tin	Na	Tin	Na	Kat	Ta	Tirkit	Dhin	Na	Dhi	Dhin	Na	

Definite Types of Theka

Tal Dadra

	×					
1.	Dha	Dhee	Na	Dha	Tee	Na
2.	Dha	Dhee	Na	Tete	Tee	Na
3.	Dhage	Dhee	Na	Dhage	Tee	Na
4.	Tirkit	Dhee	Na	Dha	Tee	Na
5.	Dha	Dhin	Dha	Dha	Tin	Ta

TAL JHAP

	×		2			0		3		
1.	Dhe	Na	Dhec	Dhee	Na	Tee	Na	Dhee	Dhee	Na

53

2.	Dhin	Nana	Dhin	Dhin	Nana	Tin	Nana	Dhin	Dhin	Nana
3.	Dhinna	Tirkit	Dhin	Dhin	Na	Tinna	Tirkit	Dhin	Dhin	Na
4.	Dhin	Tirkit	Dhee	Dhee	Na	Tin	Trikat	Dhee	Dhee	Na
5.	Dhin	Na	Dhin	Dhin	Na	Tin	Na	Dhin	Dhin	Na

Tal EK Tala

	×	0	2	0	3	4
1.	Dhin Dhin	Dhage Tirkit	Too Na	Ka Ta	Dhage Tirkit	Dhin Na
2.	Dhin dhin	Dha Dhage Tirkit	Tirkit Toona	Kat Ta	Dhage Tirkit	Dhee Na
3.	Dhin Dha dhin	Dha Tirkit	Too Na	Ka Ta	Dhage Tirkit	Dhin Na

Tal Char Tal

	×	0	2	0	3	4
1.	Dha Dha	Dhin Ta	Kit Dha	Dhin Ta	Kit Tak	Gade Gina
2.	Dhadha Dha	Din Ta	Dhage Tete	Din Ta	Tit Kat	Gade Gina
3.	Dha Tit	Din Ta	Tit Dha	Din Ta	Tit Kat	Gade Gina

Tal Teen

	×	2	0	3
1.	Na Dhee Dhee Na	Na Dhee Dhee Na	Na Tee Tee Na	Na Dhee Dha Na
2.	Dha Dhin Dhin Dha	Dha Dhin Dhin Dha	Dha Tin Tin	Ta Ta Dhin Dhin Dha
3.	Dhin Dha Dha Dhin	Dha Dhin Dhin Dha	Tin Ta Ta Tin	Dha Dhin Dhin Dha
4.	Dha Dhin — Dha	— Dha Dhin Dha	Ta Tin — Ta Dhin	Dhin Dha Dha
5.	Dha Dhin Dhin Dha	— Dha Dhin Dha Dha	Tin Tin Ta	— Dha Dhin Dha
6.	Dha Dhin — Dhin	Dha Dhin Dhin Dha Dha	Tin — Ta Ta	Dhin Dhin Dha